★

WHAT OTHERS ARE SAYING ABOUT JEFF!

"From start to finish, I was deeply moved by Jeff's Presentation. I emphasize the 'Presence' in Presentation because I felt such a depth of presence in each moment and interaction with Jeff. I was able to integrate the transformation on a personal, emotional, and spiritual level."

~ Viva Dunwoody

"Because of Jeff and his teachings, our business has soared to new heights in a timeframe we thought to be inconceivable. He helped us to transform our work culture to one of an inspired learning environment that helps us to become more effective leaders, but more importantly, empowers the staff in the office. Jeff has helped us to find meaning to what we do each day in our profession and in our personal lives. I am truly grateful for the coaching sessions we have with Jeff as he teaches us how to create simple strategies for a complex and dynamic world, strategies that lead us toward balance, toward achievements, and toward future growth both personally and professionally."

~ Lee-Ann N. Heely
Doctoral Scholar
Doctoral of Leadership Management Program
University of Phoenix, School of Advanced Studies

"Jeff has a way of inspiring me to move through and beyond the illusions that in the past have limited me."

~ Tara Alder

"As a feng shui consultant and teacher, I have used the coaching services of Jeff Bow for several years, and I can rely on him to bring out of me very good practical advice, but he also understands the need for spiritual balance. He listens deeply, and he cares deeply; he helps his clients to cultivate their true potentials in regard to their individual life's work. Through his excellent example, he has always inspired me to be more accountable to myself, my life work, and ultimately, my deeper dreams. I always think of Jeff as "a midwife for one's dreams.""

~ Kathleen Thurston, owner of Divine Order consulting

"The insight Jeff has provided me is invaluable. My business has profited immensely from Jeff's coaching, monetarily and emotionally. We've accomplished my ultimate dream in private practice. The staff now puts the patient first and the results go beyond the 'WOW' when it comes to patient care. Jeff is a life-saver. Thanks, Jeff. You're the coach we needed."

~ G.O., DDS

"Working with Jeff has given me clarity of mind to set goals and achieve those goals for my business and life. With Jeff's help I am able to ask myself questions about my business and then find solutions. Jeff holds me accountable by requesting I put my plan into action; then he follows up with me each week. I recommend Jeff's Executive Coaching to anyone who is seeking assistance setting and attaining goals by asking questions, finding solutions, and being held accountable to follow through. My business would not be where it is today in such a short amount of time without his help."

~ Kristy M, President of one of the 2010
top fifty fastest growing companies, according to *Pacific Business News*

"I've been blessed to work with Jeff on a weekly basis by having him as an individual Life Coach. I can honestly say that during the past nine months of coaching, I have not only gained insight into my professional future, but I have grown significantly as an individual. Never before have I experienced such clarity; nor have my life goals ever been as transparent as they are today.

Jeff is incredibly gifted in being able to see the individuality in all that exists, whether it is a person or circumstance. On an individual basis, Jeff's coaching has given me the insight I need to make timely and savvy life decisions that fit into my individual life style. I would highly recommend Jeff to any person who wants to gain the most out of his or her time or to those who want to achieve a higher level of personal growth."

~ Timothy C.

"I met Jeff in 1983. At that time, he was Sales Manager for a Manufacturing and supply company. I was fortunate to work under Jeff for the following eight years and followed his rise within the company to Vice President and General Manager. I always admired Jeff's ability to know each employee by name, and how he always had personal time to listen, no matter how busy he was.

I have gone to, and still go to, Jeff for help with my personal and business growth. His ability to approach a situation from beyond the normal confines of standard business allows me to learn and grow more completely than I could possibly hope for on my own.

I urge anyone considering Jeff's coaching program to take full advantage of his considerable talents, and to reap the rewards."

~ Mark F. Phipps, Kailua-Kona, Hawaii

STOP THINKING
START BELIEVING

How to Break Through Fear and Ignite Your Brilliance!

★

AVIVA
PUBLISHING
New York

JEFFERY BOW

Stop Thinking, Start Believing
How to Break Through Fear and Ignite Your Brilliance

Address all inquiries to:

Jeffery Bow
P.O. Box 390490
Keauhou, HI 96739
Telephone: (360) 929-3854
www.jeffbowcoaching.com
www.stopthinkingstartbelieving.com
www.brilliancethroughbalance.com
www.jefferybow.com

ISBN 978-1-935586-33-3

Library of Congress 2011906563

Editors: Nora Bow, Tyler Tichelaar
Cover & Interior Book Design: Fusion Creative Works

Every attempt has been made to source all quotes properly.

Printed in the United States of America

2nd Edition

For additional copies, please visit www.StopThinkingStartBelieving.com

★

DEDICATION

This book is dedicated to you the reader. May this book inspire you to find the courage to take action and live a naturally vibrant life.

★ CONTENTS ★

★

PURPOSE

I AM HERE TO SHARE THE GIFTS THAT WE ALL HAVE.
TO UNFOLD THESE TREASURES EACH AND EVERY DAY
AND TO BE IN AWE OF OUR UNIQUENESS AND BEAUTY.
WE ARE INSEPARABLE, FLUID AND FLOWING.
WE ARE ONE.

~ **Jeffery Bow**

★

INTRODUCTION

If I were fearless, I would....

I have been fortunate to meet so many amazing people throughout my life. Over the years, as an employee, I fought to be the voice for people who didn't have one with their employers. As a manager, I looked for ways to integrate people regardless of their titles or positions. As a leader, I continually searched for ways that supported companies to value people as unique individuals who added a distinctive value to the company's success.

One of the most common elements, regardless of their positions, that prevented people from solving problems, working together, creating their best lives or living their truths was fear. Fear was present at every level of the company's organizational chart and manifested its way to all parts of every person's life, including his or her home life.

This fear prevented many talented people from being promoted, having great relationships, happiness, joy, and fulfillment. It was the fear of not being good enough, of having their vulnerability exposed, of failing, of not being skilled enough, or one of the thousands of reasons that kept them trapped in an imaginary cage wanting someday to express their desire for freedom.

If this situation sounds familiar, or you know there is more to life than what you are currently experiencing, then this book is for you. It is amazing how much talent and resourcefulness lies in the untapped potential within you at this very moment. Now is your time!

Stop Thinking, Start Believing is a message to stop dwelling on thoughts that do not serve you, and instead, to believe in yourself and the possibilities that exist in the world. Thinking in the form of reflection can be beneficial for growth. However, the process of over-thinking that creates doubts about your abilities, talents, and gifts is a self-imposed roadblock to happiness. Thinking occurs in the mind. Believing comes from the heart.

Now is your time to put aside the complacency and excuses, to quit putting the dreams on hold, to stop thinking, and to start believing! It's time to break through your fears and ignite your brilliance. You already are brilliant. Now is the time to remove those masks of your brilliance that prevent you from bringing and sharing your talents and gifts to this world.

How would you complete this sentence?

If I were fearless, I would….

You may have great ideas, dreams of a better future, or goals you would like to accomplish in this lifetime. What if you were fearless? How would your life be different? What would you do differently? How would you be making a positive difference to those around you and in this world?

This book is not just about overcoming fear. It also includes: Leadership, Motivation, Inspiration, Life and Work Balance, Conflict Resolution, Change, Collaboration, and many other elements you can use as tools to support you in igniting your brilliance.

More importantly, this book is about empowering you to know you have choices. Choices to dream, create, and live a life according to your own design, your values, and your beliefs. It moves you from your head to your heart. It reinforces that you are not defined by your circumstances, but rather, what you make out of them.

This book reduces the complicated to the simple. My wish is for this book to make a positive difference in your life. You deserve a life of fun, happiness, and fulfillment. Start believing that you can make it happen. Why not start now?

With Love & Respect,

Jeffery Bow

April 19, 2011

SECTION ONE

★

VISION

★

Vision is the true creative rhythm.
~ Robert Delaunay

CHAPTER ONE

THE UNPAINTED PICTURE:
VISION

There are always flowers for those who want to see them.
~ Henri Matisse

How often have you said the words, "I'll believe it when I see it" or heard someone else say them? We have become accustomed to creating doubt rather than creating dreams. And knowing how skeptical the rest of the world is, we feel we must prove and justify ourselves in order to validate who we are so others will recognize our place in this world.

BIG DREAMS

As children, we started off with big dreams, and we had no doubt we were going to reach our dreams no matter what anyone said. We were steadfast, self-confident, honest, and determined. We knew we would find some way to succeed as we crawled on the floor or jumped on the bed or sofa and pretended we could fly with a cape. We had an expansive world, freedom to explore, unlimited imagination, and a gazillion ways to make things happen. We were persistent little buggers who were so determined to get what we wanted that we could pull out all the stops, including crying uncontrollably and playing the pity card. We bought nothing to build our forts. We were creative and had ingenuity beyond our years. Smiling, happiness, and fun were our only goals. We were in control.

WHAT WAS YOUR BIG DREAM AS A CHILD?

_____

_____

_____

_____

_____

_____

_____

_____

Today, now that you are grown, are you a reflection of doubt or do you believe if you can envision it, it can be yours? Dreaming and envisioning allow us to create a life of choice rather than living within our circumstances. With choices come self-responsibility, abundance, freedom, and the expression of your highest self. With circumstances come blame, frustration, anger, and scarcity.

WHO HAS THE MAP?

Have you ever been driving with family or friends when someone says, "Where are we?" You respond, "I don't know; I thought you knew?"An hour or two later you admit, "We're lost" and fear starts to set in as it begins to get dark.

If you were meeting friends, what would be the probability of them meeting you if they didn't know where to go? That sounds absurd, yet we let it happen to ourselves all the time. We let ourselves fall into a "wandering aimlessly," "If it's not broken, don't fix it," or "I'm fine" mindset until a crisis occurs.

Many people plan for retirement and nothing more. Retirement is a part of the financial section of your life. What about your primary relationships, self-development, extreme self-care, profession, or spirituality? If you just "go with the flow," that's okay if you are willing to accept your life as it is presented to you. Or would you be willing to spend some time creating an inspiring, creative, and fulfilling life where you determine your destination?

If you are a business owner, leader or visionary, your success is contingent on your ability to communicate your vision throughout your organization and to its end users. Having a vision that your team members can take ownership in allows them to know where the company is headed. That vision gives them hope, direction, and a sense of security. If they don't know what the vision is or where the company is headed, they will guess. When they guess, decisions made by the leadership team are often viewed as self-serving. Their lives become day-to-day experiences when they should be feeling like they are significant and inspiring contributors to the organization.

In a 1996 *Harvard Business Review* article, "Building Your Company's Vision," Jim Collins and Jerry Porras coined the term BHAG (pronounced bee-hag). A BHAG is a Big, Hairy, Audacious Goal. It is used to define visionary goals that are clear, compelling, vibrant, and engaging. Collins and Porras used this term in connection with successful companies, and later, they used it in their book *Built to Last*. Although their research led them to big corporations, the validity of the concept can be used on any size business. Following is a list of the top twenty best companies for leadership, according to the Hay Group research study[1] done for Fortune®World's Most Admired Companies®. These companies had a vision for the future that provided leadership. How many of these top twenty companies' names do you know? You know them because they are leaders in their industries, and they have kept that position because they encourage their employees through internal leadership. Their visions also inspire their employees, who then work to make the vision reality so the businesses flourish.

Top Twenty Best Companies for Leadership – April 20, 2010

1. General Electric

2. Southwest Airlines

3. 3M

4. Procter & Gamble

5. Accenture

6. Wal-Mart Stores

7. Nestle

8. Coca-Cola

9. McDonald's Corporation

---

1 Author: Mary Fontaine, Managing director, leadership and talent, Hay Group, April 20, 2010. For more information, visit: http://www.haygroup.com/BestCompaniesForLeadership/research-and-findings/global-top-20.aspx. Accessed April 17, 2011.

10. Infosys Technologies

11. IBM

12. Cisco

13. United Parcel Services (UPS)

14. IKEA

15. ABB

16. Zappos.com

17. Hewlett-Packard

18. Goldman Sachs

19. Unilever

20. General Mills, Inc

HIDDEN PARADISE

In 2003, my wife and I were looking for a lot to buy in Hawaii. One lot had been on the market for two years, so we decided to take a look at it and find out why it had not sold. We asked permission to walk on the lot so we could get an idea of what the terrain was like. It was so overgrown with trees and bushes that you could not see in front of you. The foliage was ten to twelve feet high in some places.

At first glance, it appeared that the seven-plus acres were a warehouse for weeds. As we walked the land, we realized it had a lot of character, but it had just not been maintained. It had potential. We felt the reason it had not sold was because whoever had looked at it previously had only seen it at face value. They had not taken the time to engage themselves by walking on the property and envisioning its potential.

Eventually, we purchased the lot and hired a contractor to come in and clear away the brush. Once the clearing was completed, it revealed a beautiful park-like setting with macadamia nut and coffee trees. Neighbors who stopped by the lot could not believe what they saw. This transformation happened because we took the time to engage ourselves in the process and visualize the manifestation of the property's potential.

WHO SWITCHED THE WORD?

The words "dream" and "vision" appear to be interchangeable. Somewhere along the way, as we got older, the word "dream" turned into the word "vision." It came into play, perhaps, because it sounded more businesslike and more legitimate, while "dream" was associated with daydreaming or being a dreamer, which meant not taking action to make the vision come true. However, both words really have positive connotations and are worth valuing.

The ability to dream and visualize allows us to explore beyond the confines of our normal everyday life without risk. The more we dream and visualize, the more ideas we will have to move us beyond what presently confines us. For example, it's well known that people need to be exposed to a product or service on average five to seven times before they will make a purchase. Similarly, the more exposure we have to a thought, an idea, or a process, the more we become comfortable with it until it passes from an idea or dream to being a truth or action we no longer need to think about it.

Before you learned to ride a bike, you may have seen others kids riding bikes, or seen a bicycle at the store or in an advertisement. You were motivated to get a bike and ride it, even if you'd never ridden before. You were already picking out the colors and style in your mind. Do you remember when you got onto your first bike how uneasy or unbalanced you may have felt? You may have had training wheels as a sense of security in the beginning, but once those training wheels came off and you were riding successfully on your own, do you remember that feeling of exhilaration taking over? Once you got used to riding your bike all the time, you could just jump on the bike and go without having to think about balancing, pedaling, or braking. Riding a bike became natural.

Similarly, when you regularly dream and visualize, doing so becomes natural. When you dream and visualize often, picturing yourself in your vision and forming mental images along with the accompanying emotions you would like to experience, you trigger your brain to believe what you envision is possible, which then encourages you to make it happen.

> *Vision is the art of seeing what is invisible to others.*
> ~ Jonathan Swift

In 1952, Roger Bannister, the sprinter, decided to set a new goal after a disappointing fourth place finish in the Olympics. His new goal was to run a four-minute mile. No one had ever accomplished such a feat. On May 6, 1954, at the Iffley Road track in Oxford, he set a new record of 3 minutes, 59.4

seconds. What was more amazing was that once he broke the record, others followed in his tracks. Just forty-six days later, John Landy of Australia beat his record with a run of 3 minutes, 57.9 seconds. Once Bannister set the new world record, Landy saw it was possible to break the four-minute mile barrier, which allowed him to envision new possibilities.

WHAT IS THE DIFFERENCE BETWEEN VISION AND GOALS?

Having a vision is the ability to have a vivid, imaginative concept that is sensory-rich and engaging. Having a vision allows goals to come alive before a goal is set. Goals have a termination point, but visions continually morph and change to meet the inspiration of their creator. Having a vision becomes a lifestyle.

Have you ever set goals in the past and never reached them? Most of us have! When I fall short, it feels worse than when I started. For example, I once had a goal to retire by the time I was thirty-five. I thought that if I were retired, I wouldn't have to work. Work at that point in my life was just that...work. It was a termination point. When thirty-five came and went, I started to compare myself to others and where I "should" be in life. I didn't realize at the time that one component was missing from my goal setting...visualizing.

Visualizing or having a vision creates an environment that's conducive for goals to thrive. It's like gardening. Visualizing prepares the garden bed for the goals to be planted as seeds. The more sensory perception, "nutrients," we add to the process, the richer the soil. When goals have rich soil, they thrive. Then, magic happens.

HOW DOES HAVING A VISION APPLY TO YOU?

I believe we each have a responsibility to ourselves and to our Source of Divine Presence to live the best and most vibrant life we can. Regardless of what we do, our position at work, or where we are in our lives, we have the ability to set an intention for what we want, to visualize it, and to manifest our ultimate dreams.

The ability to envision your future means you can consciously create your environment rather than letting your circumstances lead your life. You can look at where you want to be, not where you are.

VISUALIZING

At the end of this chapter is an eight-step exercise to guide you in writing down your vision. In creating your vision of how magnificent you want your life to be, make sure you consider all aspects of your life, including:

- Your Profession
- Your Primary Relationship
- Secondary Relationships
- Finances
- Spirituality
- Self-Improvement
- Physical Surroundings
- Rest and Relaxation
- Extreme Self-Care

If these words do not resonate with you, you can change them to something that does, and add or subtract any others that may be of value to you. You want to make sure your vision provides balance in your life so you are not overwhelmed, even by too much good. More will be covered about life balance in Chapter 8: Brilliance through Balance.

Generally speaking, there are different levels of visions. Your preference for timeframes to turn your vision into reality, or for what may be short- or long-term goals to make the vision come true, may differ. General definitions may be:

Short-term: less than one year

Long-term: greater than one year

"Laser vision" or Focus: specific and task-focused.

Short-Term Vision

A short-term vision is excellent for helping to break down your largest most audacious dream. Looking at where you are in your life, and comparing it to your highest potential, may be overwhelming at first. A short-term vision allows you to "chunk it down" into smaller, more manageable bits. Accomplishing small bits of your vision will help you to build confidence and reduce the fear and intimidation you may feel about your awesome dream.

Not "chunking it down" would be like having a vision to be a tri-athlete but never having run more than two miles or never to have gone swimming without a noodle (a flotation device that looks like a noodle). As absurd as it may seem, we often do fail to break down our dreams into manageable parts; then we feel overwhelmed, become disappointed, and give up.

In the examples above, a first small step could be to extend your running from two to three miles, or you may start to swim a short distance in a pool without the noodle. What would be your first small step to make your vision become reality?

Long-Term Vision

Let your long-term vision be wide open for your interpretation. One of the things to remember is that your vision will be for this point and time in your life. It represents your current aspirations, hopes, and dreams. There is no wrong way to create your vision, and it will change and evolve as you do.

Create your wildest, ultimate, inspiring, sensual, and juicy vision, dripping with all the emotions you will feel when you are living in that reality. Incorporate all the senses: touch, taste, smell, feeling, seeing, and even your sixth sense of intuition. Dedicate the time to write down what your ultimate life would look like, and use as many sheets of paper as you need to capture the essence of where you would love to be in this lifetime.

Laser Vision or Focus

A laser vision is usually specific and task-oriented. It addresses an immediate need and brings all your attention at that moment to resolving the issue. As an example, if the water pipe broke in your house, you would immediately come up with the steps first to stop it, and then decide how to get it fixed. All your attention is focused on the issue at hand.

EXERCISE: DREAM SHIELD/VISION BOARD

Create a visual representation of your collective thoughts, dreams, aspirations, and ultimate life. A vision board is something that will stimulate the senses and inspire you to keep moving forward every day.

I was introduced to this process by Kathleen Thurston, a Feng Shui consultant who later became my friend. I have found it to be an effective tool in the visionary process, and because you can be creative in how you construct the Vision Board, it is helpful and conducive to different people's ways of learning. I invite you to try this process.

<u>You will need the following supplies</u>:

    a. A foam core or other rigid board approximately 20" wide x 32" high. The board can really be any size, but my thought is the bigger the dream, the bigger the board. Get whatever size will fit in your car or will fit where you want to place it in your home or office.

    b. A lot of magazines you like.

    c. Scissors.

    d. Glue. (A rubber cement type product works well.)

    e. Marking pens to draw or write.

    f. Music. (Optional.)

<u>How to get started</u>:

    1. Set aside approximately two hours where you will not be disturbed and can dedicate this time completely to yourself. If you decide to do this process with a partner, there

should be no talking or sharing of supplies except the magazines. Shut off your cell phone. No talking includes any comments, good or bad, about anyone's board. There is no wrong way to do this process. Whatever you do, it will be perfect!

2. If you decide to have music, put on your favorite music. Find a comfortable spot on the floor, table, or wherever you can spread out.

3. Look through the magazines to find pictures, words, or anything that resonates with you. Cut or tear them out.

4. You can paste what you cut out onto your board as you find the items, or collect all the items to arrange and paste later. Arrange your images, sayings, drawings, or write on your board according to whatever inspires or moves you. Note: You can have as many or as few images as you want. Remember, your vision board is your creation.

5. After you have completed the board, place it in a spot where you can look and feel the essence of what you have created. This step is really important, so take as much time as you need. In the hustle and bustle of life, to take the time really to value who you are and the life you want to live is critical in anchoring your intended vision.

6. On the back of the board, write your name, the date, and the place of creation.

My first vision board had a huge impact on me. It revealed the life of the person who had long struggled to get out of me—my authentic self. At the time, it had been about two years since I had left my job in a corporate environment, where I had been a vice-president and general manager with all the benefits. I had been in the middle of building my house when I left my job with no other job lined up.

It was February 15th, 2003. My wife and I had just finished our vision boards. We had each taken the time to reflect privately on our works of art. In the middle of my board was a large tree with a woman surrounding it. I had placed a picture of a young boy pouring water over his head, bathing in the traditional Japanese way, done prior to soaking in a furo, a Japanese soaking tub. I kept staring at my board until my wife asked me whether she could look at my board. After I nodded, "Yes," she looked for a while, and then she asked me whether I realized I was represented by the boy at the root of the tree and that everything extended out from me. I reflected for a second; then all of a sudden, I started weeping. Although I had always fought for those who felt they had no voice and had tried to dissolve the barriers between management and employees, it was only at that moment that I realized I actually had the ability to influence people in a positive way.

> *All truth passes through three stages.*
> *First, it is ridiculed. Second, it is violently opposed.*
> *Third, it is accepted as being self-evident.*
> ~ Arthur Schopenhauer

THE BUSINESS VISION BOARD

How often do you walk into an office and see the owner or manager's picture on the wall? Imagine if you walked in and saw Vision Boards created by the individuals, teams, and leaders together. What would your thoughts be about the company then? Engaging the workforce and taking ownership in the vision of a company is a tremendous motivational tool that builds cohesiveness and creates an environment where people can thrive personally and professionally. When people thrive, so does your business.

SIMPLE STEPS TO START WRITING YOUR DREAMS OR VISION

Here are eight steps to jump start your next big dream.

1. Create a vision.

Where do you want to be? Create the biggest, most audacious vision you can think of and make it *juicy*. Make it dripping juicy so you can sense, feel, and experience all the emotions that go along with experiencing your dream.

Without a vision, we let our circumstances create our life. With a vision, we create our circumstances. In a business, a shared vision allows all the team players to know where the company is headed and what their future holds. Without this vision for the future, life for the team becomes a routine and day-to-day experience.

2. Incorporate all parts of your life.

When creating an exciting and fabulous business vision, imagine how other aspects of your life will be incorporated. As an example, if you have children, a spouse or partner, how do you see them in this jaw-dropping life you are creating?

3. Write it down—Legitimize yourself!

Pick a time when you will not be interrupted. Turn on your favorite music (or not) and write down an unedited, ultimate, juicy, sensual, and moving description of your vision. Remember, the vision you write down is for this point of time in your life, and you can change it in the future.

4. Incorporate what motivates you.

If you are inspired by a quote, a picture or an article, keep that with your written vision.

5. Chunk it down.

Many great ideas, leading edge technology, and magnificent companies were never created because the dream was so big that the creator did not know how to manage it. Trying to jump from concept to realization is like trying to light a big log in the fireplace with a match. I invite you to start with the kindling. Break down your vision into smaller and more manageable pieces. What is your kindling?

6. Create your road map.

Using your intuition and knowledge, plan how you are going to get to where you would like to be. Seek out advice. Get involved in groups and events in your field of interest. Some people like to use the intention and manifestation process and let things happen organically. Some like to write a plan. Remember that your plan doesn't have to be 50-100 pages long. It can be one or two pages or whatever serves you.

7. Do something—anything!

Every day, do something that works on getting you closer to your vision. Some things may seem small, but they may turn into big, brilliant fires that will ignite your passion. Start your day fueling your passion.

8. Acknowledge your progress.

Don't let bumps in the road define who you are. Keep moving forward. I bet that, right now, you are already doing things toward fulfilling your vision. Take the time to acknowledge yourself for things you are doing every day toward your vision.

A former milkshake machine salesman, Ray Kroc, saw the potential to sell more mixers with every new restaurant that opened. Inspired by that vision, at the age of fifty-nine, Ray purchased a company that we know today as McDonald's. The rest is history.

It's never too late. You can accomplish anything you want in life and at any age.

CHAPTER TWO

INTENTION/MANIFESTATION

When you set an intention, when you commit, the entire universe conspires to make it happen.
~ Sandy Forster

Have you ever dreamed of a better life? Have you pictured in your mind your ideal home, surroundings, soulmate, or job? It is possible to achieve these things if you believe you can. There is a timeless law of the universe that exists and it happens all around you.

The movies *The Secret* (2006) and *What the Bleep Do We Know!?* (2004) brought to light that everyone has the ability to create his or her reality through the process of intention and manifestation. Whether you know it or not, you have already experienced this process in many ways.

For example, have you ever thought of getting a parking space close to the front of the store when the parking lot was packed full of cars, and then, magically, a space opened up for you? You may have discounted this event as just luck the first and maybe even the second time it happened, but as time went on, you realized that it was more than luck. You created that opportunity so it could happen.

The power of thought is a wonderful gift that everyone has, but one that not many believe in, understand, or use. While many definitions exist for the Law of Intention and Manifestation, here is my simple definition: Intention and manifestation mean, **"Turning thought into reality."**

RECOGNIZE YOUR BRILLIANCE

Think of three other instances when something you thought about materialized.

1. _____
   _____
   _____

2. _____
   _____
   _____

3. _____
   _____
   _____

THE MENTAL DIET

Emmett Fox, in his book *Power Through Constructive Thinking*, posed a challenge in his chapter, "The Seven Day Mental Diet." Fox challenges us to focus only on positive thoughts for seven days. If you harbored a negative thought, situation, or event for more than a couple of minutes, you would have to start over again at the beginning. This exercise is one of the most powerful I have ever experienced! It made me realize how much of my time was wasted on thoughts that did not serve me in realizing my ultimate vision.

I encourage you to take a look at how often you let negative thoughts enter your thinking and speaking. Our society plays and encourages drama (drama = negativity) to get people's attention. How does the world of drama serve you in your own vision and life dreams? Do you focus on the 98 percent in your life that's working or the 2 percent that's not?

True intention and manifestation embody a win-win situation for everyone directly and indirectly involved. It is easy, fluid, and flowing. It does not incorporate fear, scarcity, power over others, or taking advantage of others. As evident as this process may be, people fail to believe they have the ability to manifest, so they try to control others by using force or unethical means to get what they want, and it's usually at the expense of others.

2005 HARLEY CUSTOM SUPER GLIDE

In 2005, I decided to take a motorcycle safety class. I had taken the class ten years prior, but I had never followed through getting a license. It was something I felt I had left unfinished. So, in late 2005, I finally completed the class and got my license. I hadn't given much thought yet about what kind of motorcycle I might get since my goal was to complete the course and get a license.

Later while creating a vision board, I put a picture of a Honda motorcycle on it to represent my intention of getting a bike. As time went on, I couldn't find one that I really liked so my wife asked, "Have you ever thought of a Harley?" I felt Harleys were lacking in the latest technology, but I told her I would look into it. Finally, after reading the reviews, evaluating the price, and making sure I liked how it looked, I decided on a 2005 Harley Dyna Custom Super Glide. Harley's glossy foldout picture of a black cherry-colored bike with all its chrome was what finally convinced me it was the one. Every night I went over the picture brochure as if it were a treasure map. Finally one night, my wife said, "If that's the bike you want, then perhaps you could change the picture on the vision board. So I copied the picture on the brochure and put it on the vision board.

The following day when we headed to Oahu, Hawaii, (we lived in Kona, Hawaii at the time), my wife asked whether I wanted to stop by Harley Davidson and buy a motorcycle. I replied, "Only if they have the exact one I'm looking for." As we perused the motorcycles on the showroom floor, I didn't see the bike I was looking for, so I asked the salesman whether the dealership carried it.

After he checked his computer, he asked us to follow him. We continued behind him as he unlocked doors and took us to the top floor with glass windows that could be seen by cars as they passed by on the freeway. On a revolving display was a black cherry 2005 Dyna Custom Super Glide. We bought the bike that day and had it shipped home.

This personal example demonstrates just how powerful our thoughts and intentions can be. In sharing this story and other examples, my hope is that people see the power they have within, in the present moment, to manifest and create a life that is vibrant, happy, and fulfilling.

WHAT REALLY IS INTENTION AND MANIFESTATION?

I defined Intention and Manifestation earlier as **"Turning thought into reality."** They are the creation of something that doesn't appear to exist, and making it a tangible, sensory rich experience. This process is the same as when someone who has an idea turns it into a reality. Ray Kroc who envisioned McDonald's, Colonel Sanders of Kentucky Fried Chicken, and the owners of Costco all started with a thought.

In my own journey, I have found the following elements or steps in the process. See if you can identify with these. You can add your own steps as well.

1. Have an idea, vision, or dream. Know the concept of what you want.

2. Embody "knowing that you already have it" and that it is manifesting as you think of it. If you instead focus on being in a "wanting" state, then you send the message to the universe that you do not have it and that message comes from a place of lack rather than abundance, so the universe responds by thinking you do not want it.

3. Release the how, where, and when of your vision.

4. Release any expectations.

5. Know that the universe conspires in your favor.

6. Take action. (This step may seem contradictory toward the intention and manifestation process, but it is one of the most important.)

ACTION – HOW DOES ACTION REALLY PLAY INTO THE PROCESS?

Two twin brothers, Skip and Jack, lived in a remote area accessible only by four-wheel drive. They lived a mile apart in the Pacific Northwest. Both of them owned four-wheel drive vehicles that were capable of moving easily through the snow. Skip and Jack were smart, spiritual, and loving people raised by good parents. They both believed in the intention and manifestation process.

During a snowstorm, Skip and Jack both were running out of food and lost their electricity. They imagined having a bowl of hot soup, their pantries stocked to ride out the storm, and the smells of their favorite meal cooking on the stove.

Skip decided that if his intentions were powerful enough, he would soon have a bounty of food to stock his pantry. Jack looked forward to having a great meal with a nice bowl of clam chowder and bread, so he decided to set the intention of receiving a bounty of supplies and food. Jack called Skip to see whether he wanted to join him to set out to the nearby store. Skip said that he had set his intention and didn't need to go anywhere; help was on its way. Skip insisted that Jack do the same and wait it out. Jack had the knowing (intention) that his pantry was as good as stocked, but he wanted to head toward the store while there was still daylight.

Jack headed out on his ten-mile trek, encountering the usual beautiful sights that accompany a fresh snowfall. Snow dusted cedars, firs, and pines hovered over deer, squirrels, and birds foraging for food. As he passed abandoned cars along the way that were stuck in the snow, he came upon a stranded couple and offered them a ride. They lived about halfway to the country store at the 5.5-mile marker. Upon reaching the 5-mile marker, a huge tree had fallen across the road and blocked the path. The couple, Nancy and Bill, mentioned that they lived only a half mile away so the three of them got out and started walking to their house. As they approached, Jack noticed that they lived on a beautiful farm. Although snow covered most of the area, Jack could see what a well manicured and cared for property it was.

The couple invited him in and insisted that he stay for lunch. They were so appreciative that he had stopped to give them a ride that they wanted to thank him by preparing a home cooked meal. As Nancy sat and talked with Jack, Bill, being the gourmet cook, headed to the kitchen to prepare lunch.

Jack began to smell the aroma of fresh baked bread and soon lunch was ready. As Jack walked over to the table, he saw a beautiful presentation of clam chowder served in a homemade bread bowl. The meal was everything Jack had imagined and intended for himself.

In their discussions, Nancy and Bill discovered that Jack was headed to the store to get supplies and food. After lunch, they led Jack to a storage building close to their house. As they opened the door, Jack thought he was entering a supermarket. There were walls lined with shelves of canned goods, and refrigerators stocked with everything one could imagine. In addition to their farm, Nancy and Bill were wholesale distributors for natural and organic foods and supplies. They invited Jack to stock up on whatever he needed. Jack offered to pay them, but Nancy and Bill would not hear of it. They let Jack know that so many others had passed them by while he was the only one who had stopped and offered them a ride. They wanted to return the favor.

Bill later took Jack back to his car on a tractor along with his food and supplies. Bill removed the tree, plowed the road, and waved in gratitude as he drove off. Jack waved goodbye in astonishment at the luck he had just experienced in meeting the couple.

Skip was still at home waiting.

LIFE IS NOT STATIC

Intention and manifestation work through movement. Movement of energy, thought, and action. From the example above, Skip's inaction did not get him anywhere.

Life moves on whether or not we want it to. Hanging on to the past prevents you from moving forward in your life, and it also hinders the intention and manifestation process from taking place. Bringing your past into the present and not letting go is like locking yourself to an imaginary ball and chain you drag around. The more you hang onto the past, the more weight is added. This weight is what prevents you from moving forward.

How does not letting go of the past affect the intention and manifestation process? You may miss the opportunities in front of you because as life moves forward, you are straddled by the weight of your past holding you back. Releasing the burdens of the past allows you to be present and to experience what life has to offer.

EXERCISE: RELEASING THE PAST

What have you been holding on to from the past that you would like to release? Release it now and declare it done.

I finally would like to let go of:

_____

_____

_____

_____

_____

_____

_____

_____

_____

_____

_____

_____

_____

_____

WHAT INTENTION AND MANIFESTATION ARE NOT

When people learn something new, they have a tendency to have it consume their world. What you focus on expands. That is a good thing, right? Be careful that, as you begin to take on this new awareness of Intention and Manifestation, it does not become a catch all solution not only to your own problems but others' problems as well. For example, a person who was just in a car accident will not appreciate it if you say to him, "You attracted that. What thoughts were going through your mind?"

More likely, the person was just not paying attention at that moment, and that lack of attention, not his thoughts, was what led to the accident.

Our thoughts alone are not the sole determiner of our reality. Here are some examples that demonstrate that we do not create the intention for and manifest everything in our world.

- Terminal illness in infants and young children
- All people affected by the tragic events of 9-11
- People affected by natural disasters. For example, the people in Thailand affected by the tsunami; the people of Haiti, China, Japan, and other parts of the world affected by earthquakes.
- People involved in accidents
- Innocent bystanders who are affected by a crime

SUMMARY

The intention and manifestation process is a tool for you to use that helps you to focus on what you want rather than what you don't want. It keeps you in a positive state of mind and lends itself to **self-responsibility.** Self-responsibility requires reflection of your actions, including thoughts to take control of your life and create your circumstances. Maya Angelou, in a master class series, reflected, "Make something of the situation that you were given" as she discussed her life and the challenges she faced growing up.

WHAT INTENTION DO YOU HAVE THAT YOU WOULD LIKE TO MANIFEST AT THIS TIME?

_____

_____

_____

_____

_____

_____

_____

_____

_____

_____

_____

_____

_____

_____

_____

_____

_____

_____

_____

_____

_____

_____

_____

_____

_____

_____

_____

_____

CHAPTER THREE

WHAT WE FOCUS ON EXPANDS!

*The key to success is to focus our conscious mind
on things we desire not things we fear.*
~ Brian Tracy

Have you ever heard the saying, "Don't make a mountain out of a mole hill"? It is a cliché used when describing an act of turning something small into something big. It is used to describe a situation of exaggeration, such as how a lawyer could take the smallest detail or a word someone said and expand it into having a certain meaning to prove a point. **How many mountains have you made from mole hills?**

Expanding what you focus on can help or hinder you. You have the ability to expand something in any way you choose. It is a skill few people know about and even fewer use to their advantage. You can use this powerful skill to enhance your life. Notice the contrast in expanding in the two examples below.

<u>Situation #1:</u> Do you remember wanting to get the car of your dreams? It might have been your first car as a teenager or your first brand new car. For me, it was a '67 Camaro! Your focus was on that car. You kept pictures and magazines where you could look at it all the time. As you looked around, as if by

magic, more and more of those cars were around. You started to notice your dream car passing you by, in magazines or in car shows. The same color, make, and model. It was as if owning one were meant to be. The more you focused on the car, the more you saw it on the road. It expanded your thoughts, reinforced your dream, and made the possibility of buying that car all the more compelling.

When you focused your attention on that specific car, your mind became like a radar, scanning, searching, looking for any suspects that matched the description. The scanning took place in your subconscious, so when you saw the car, it was a surprise. The cars just seemed to appear, but in reality the cars were always there; you just hadn't noticed them before because you hadn't been focused on that particular car.

Situation #2: Society's preoccupation with "drama" in the news, current reality shows, and advertising make it easy for us to be lured into drama's grasp. When we give into the fear the media creates or the importance advertising places on looking a certain way or having a certain product, we allow our thoughts to focus on self-imposed limitations for growth in all areas of our lives. At times, watching these shows can be fun, relaxing, and entertaining, but how much influence do they have on us subconsciously? Do you find yourself focusing on the little things that are not working, such as someone else's annoying habit because a similar habit was pointed out on a reality show? Do you focus on not having a product that will make your skin look better rather than on how nice the rest of you looks? All of a sudden, the little things become the main focus in your life.

If you start to find that little things are bothering you, that you are making mountains out of molehills, and you are blaming other people, situations, or circumstances for your unhappiness, then it's time to step back and focus on what is working.

PAINTING RUBBISH CANS

I experienced how awareness can work when I was in the sixth grade, although I didn't understand the concept at the time. I attended a small school tucked away on Oahu in a valley called Hahaione. The neighborhood was just developing, so we knew most of the people around us and from the neighboring towns.

I was running for president of our student body and had to do something for my campaign. At twelve years old, my ideas were simple. I came up with the idea, along with my campaign managers and friends, to paint the rubbish cans (in Hawaii, garbage cans were called rubbish cans). We felt that if people saw painted rubbish cans with designs, they would be attracted to them, and therefore, use them instead of littering. Eventually, I became class president. I am not sure if my idea of painting the rubbish cans was the key to our success, but it definitely brought attention to ways to beautify our school.

Looking back now, I could say that I changed the focus of the student body by bringing the students' awareness to the prevention of litter and inspiring them to take that thought to create a more beautiful environment. Wow, it was so much simpler to explain in the sixth grade!

LEARNING AND EDUCATION

I have been blessed in my life to meet Peter J. Reding, creator of The Foundation for Inspired Learning. Peter recognized that people have an innate sense for learning, so he changed the philosophy of learning from a critique base to an acknowledgment base, celebrating what the learner has already learned. This program focused on the best learning method for individuals and the conditions that allow learning to thrive.

Peter used the premise *"What we focus on expands,"* meaning what we bring our attention to, we get more of. He created an alternative method that is conducive to people of all ages thriving in a learning environment. The Inspired Learning Model™ has helped to change thousands of lives, including mine.

This pioneering model creates an environment that is non-threatening, inspiring, motivating, and empowers the learner to focus on learning, growth, and success.

> ***What We Focus on Expands—***
> ***applied in a professional setting***

THE BACKGROUND

I had been working with a dentist who had a relatively new staff for a couple of years. During that time, the dentist had been aligning his team with his mission and vision, and in the process, he continued to filter out anyone who wasn't a good fit. The practice had six people including the dentist.

The dentist originally chose his profession because he wanted to have a positive impact on it and to create a place where, through education and example, the fear of dentistry would be minimized or eliminated.

THE NEED

The dentist's practice and patient count were growing at a rapid pace. The need to have continual training and cross training on a regular basis was of the utmost importance. So he started weekly morning training sessions for the entire staff. Actual hands-on training was done, so everyone had a chance to observe, learn, and perform.

THE OPPORTUNITY

During the training program, the doctor and the office administrator noticed the number of mistakes that were being made. It didn't seem like their training and retention practices were resulting in much improvement, and in the process, it appeared the staff members were making more and more mistakes. The current method of training was to identify people's mistakes, correct them on the spot, and have them redo the procedure.

The opportunity here was to connect the doctor and the staff and create a method that would be inspiring and conducive to their learning.

THE PROPOSAL

When this situation was brought to me in the form of frustration, I asked the dentist and his office manager whether they were open to exploring a different mindset and method in how they trained their staff. Would they accept a challenge that may have contradicted what they were taught in school and in their professional training? They eagerly accepted the challenge.

I presented the idea: *What we focus on expands.* I had them apply this concept to their current training and think about the type of results they were receiving. Immediately, the light bulbs went on. The bottom line was that if you focus on the mistakes, you get more mistakes. The good news was that you could use the idea of *what we focus on expands* in a positive light.

The proposal was to change their training from focusing on staff mistakes to focusing on what they were doing right; these successes were to be acknowledged immediately, not only by the dentist and the office manager, but by the staff members' peers. Everyone had to look for an authentic acknowledgment that was different than what others were saying. Now, their focus was on expanding and celebrating the successes of each individual.

THE RESULT

Two weeks later when I met with the dentist and office manager, I was told, "You wouldn't believe what's happening in our training! The staff is excelling and is also now making suggestions on how to improve the processes."

Changing the focus in their trainings had allowed them to get the desired results and more. Once they focused on what the staff was doing correctly and were able to expand that, they continually received more of that. **What they focused on expanded!!!**

WHERE WAS YOUR FOCUS WHEN YOU
WERE DATING OR IN AWE OF SOMEONE?

Think back to a time when you were dating or maybe as a teenager when you had a crush on an actor or a rock star.

When you were dating and had an interest in someone, your focus was 100 percent on that person. That person could only do everything right. The object of your affection was your prince or princess or maybe your knight in shining armor. You doted on his or her every move, word, and action. The person could do no wrong. Today, you may think your fascination with that person was only hormones, that he or she represented something new and fresh, or it was just excitement. Whatever the reason, your focus was all positive. Even when your friends may have questioned your choice, you were steadfast and determined that he/she was the perfect match for you.

As time went on and you were together for a while, you began to notice the person's little annoying habits. You may have gone from a 100 percent positive focus to being 99 percent positive and 1 percent negative. You kept what you were noticing to yourself, but more and more, you began to notice how much those habits really bothered you. Then, you started to notice other things about the person, something he or she said or did, or didn't do. Maybe as a woman, you got flowers and little gifts all the time when you first met, but now only once in a great while.

Your focus on the relationship turned to those things that were not going right. Your focus changed from 99 percent positive and 1 percent negative to 75 percent positive and 25 percent negative. The more you focused on the negative, the more it seemed to grow. Your focus was expanding in the wrong direction. Often in these cases, as you may well know, the result is that the partners begin to have disagreements and the relationship ended all because the people in the relationship changed their focus.

PAUL NEWMAN AND JOANNE WOODWARD'S MARRIAGE

Paul Newman and Joanne Woodward's marriage lasted fifty years before Paul Newman passed away from cancer. Their marriage was one of the most famous marriages in Hollywood and a miracle by today's standards. How did their marriage manage to last for so long? Here is what they both said about it:

> Joanne said she was "married to the most considerate, romantic man." "We are very, very different people and yet somehow we fed off those varied differences, and instead of separating us, it has made the whole bond a lot stronger."[1]

> Paul says that their marriage lasted because of "great impatience tempered by patience. When you have been together this long, sometimes you drive each other nuts, but underneath that is some core of affection and respect."[2]

It would have been easy for this couple to focus on their differences or what wasn't working, but instead they chose to focus on what was working and had a wonderful relationship during their life together. Their commitment to each other in mar-

1 "Paul Newman and wife Joanne celebrate 50 years of marriage." Hellomagazine.com. January 29, 2008.
2 Griffin, Nancy. "Newman's Luck." *AARP*. May & June 2005.

riage was not taken lightly. They were committed to making their relationship a priority, and they continually worked to strengthen the bond between them. Their commitment to each other was a true sign of respecting each other's individuality and honoring that in their relationship.

I wonder how many marriages and relationships would be saved simply by the partners changing their focus from the negative to the positive aspects of the other person and committing to doing everything possible to make the relationship work. Maybe together we can improve the success rate of long-term committed relationships worldwide.

PERSPECTIVE

We can always choose to perceive things differently.
You can focus on what's wrong in your life,
or you can focus on what's right.
~ Marianne Williamson

When I was about four years old, we had a huge grassy hill in the back of our house. My brother, sister, and I came up with great plans to use it as a sledding hill. We crafted our sleds out of cardboard and had a whirl of a time, pushing, pulling, and sliding. With no cares in the world and no bills to pay, our focus was on having fun! We found every way to have fun sliding down that hill. As redundant as it may seem, we never got bored with our adventures. The thought never entered our minds. Our focus was on having fun and more of it.

We eventually moved away from that house. As time passed, the memories remained. I revisited my old neighborhood many years later and discovered that the "huge hill" in back of the house was not very big. As an adult, my perspective is different. When I was four, it was a "huge hill" and that was my focus. In my mind, I expanded the hill or it might have been relative to my size as a child.

As I reflected, my thoughts began to expand to the great neighborhood I grew up in and the people we called aunts and uncles (people close to us but not blood related). My focus was not on how small the hill was, but rather, the fond memories that shaped who I am today.

MAKE A CHOICE

The most wonderful thing in life is that we have the ability to make choices. Regardless of our circumstances or life history, we can have the life we desire. Is our glass half-empty or half-full? It's a simple metaphor for our perspectives, but it also is a determinate for how your view of life will predict your future. It is your choice whether you decide to view the glass as half-empty or half-full.

IT'S NOT JUST RAH, RAH, RAH!

Focusing on what is working and having a positive outlook doesn't deny the fact that problems exist. Traffic is something I hear about often, and people usually express frustration when they talk about it. Traffic, however, is an example of something we cannot change. So, we have a choice—we can grumble every fifteen seconds about how the traffic isn't moving; we can complain about the driver who lets someone get in front of him, or we can use the time to listen to audio books, great music on CDs, or the radio.

It doesn't matter what happened in the past. It's about moving forward. We can learn something from every situation. We can look for varieties of solutions and find the opportunity in every problem. Give yourself every reason to succeed and live a vibrant life.

Having the courage to use your ability to expand what you focus on in a progressive and productive way not only supports who you are and what you stand for, but it also helps to make this world we live in a better place.

Take a look at the legendary Stevie Wonder. Born prematurely in 1950, he was blind nearly from birth. He began playing instruments at an early age and sang in the choir. Stevie went on to become an icon in the music industry, recording over thirty Top Ten hits and winning two Grammys, the Lifetime Achievement Award, the Academy Award for Best Song, and selling over 100 million records. He has also received numerous other accolades and awards.[3]

Stevie Wonder's impact upon the music industry and the world has been phenomenal. Numerous other musicians and songwriters have been inspired by his music and his ability to write and sing complex songs that included key changes and extended chord use. In addition to his ability to write and sing music, he played a myriad of instruments.

It would have been easy for Stevie to play the victim card. Instead, he chose to focus his attention on creating and expanding his musical abilities.

3 http://en.wikipedia.org/wiki/Stevie_Wonder. Accessed April 12, 2011.

For all of us who have doubts and fears about bringing who we are into the limelight, remember the great Stevie Wonder, who to this day continues to light up the world.

THE EXPANDING UNIVERSE

There is much for us to learn about the universe that surrounds us. Maybe that's why so many of us are interested in UFO's. The mystique that exists is phenomenal when it comes to exploring outer space. Is there life on other planets? Can we survive on other planets? Science fiction movies explore these possibilities and expand our imaginations and our mindset.

The United States and several other countries have dedicated space programs to explore the universe. On July 20, 1969, Neil Armstrong and Buzz Aldrin were the first humans to walk on the moon. It seemed as if the world stopped for the moment. I was nine years old at the time, and I remember the momentous impact that event had on our country and the world. The cartoon *The Jetsons* was now a real possibility. Think back to how old you were and what was happening in your life and world at that time. You may not have even been born yet. Computers were not mainstream at that time and cell phones did not exist. Technology was not as advanced as it is today, but because of a focus on space exploration, the United States was the first to accomplish the walk on the moon.

Astronomy and the universe are great examples of how *what we focus on expands*. As telescopes increase in power, astronomers are finding new planets and galaxies that were thought just to be stars. In the last ten years, the Hubble Telescope has expanded our ability to rethink the universal landscape and its creation theories.[4] As new telescopes increase in power with the ability to zoom in closer, we are able to expand our previously thought constraints and explore areas in the universe beyond our solar system. Scientists are finding that there is an infinite universe just waiting to be discovered.

What "You" Focus on Expands

You are the center of your own universe. You have the ability to create your world and to focus on where you would like to be in this lifetime. If you want to make a difference in the world, then once you set your focus on it, the universe will align and help you to get there. We are the limits of our boundaries. We set our own capacity to expand, enlighten, and engage.

Harland Sanders, at the age of sixty-five, found himself penniless. He went on the road to sell his chicken to restaurants, trying to get them to buy his seasoning packets. Legend has it that Sanders received 1,009 "No's" before he heard his first "Yes." He knew that if he could get people to use his seasoning packets, they would love the chicken. Ever since then, "The Colonel" is known for his eleven secret herbs and spices and his restaurant franchise Kentucky Fried Chicken (KFC) has become internationally known.

Colonel Sanders focused on always looking ahead, not looking back at the rejections he received. He didn't look at how old he was and what he didn't accomplish. Colonel Sanders kept looking at all the opportunities to sell seasoning packets.

4 For more information, visit www.hubblesite.org.

You too can keep looking for all the opportunities to bring your innate gifts and passion to this world.

SCARCITY VS. ABUNDANCE

It's easy to get caught up in a scarcity mode when you have just enough money to pay the bills and get by. However, by focusing on what you do have, and by believing and knowing that there is always plenty to go around, you will notice that you will begin to receive more and more.

RECOGNIZING YOUR BRILLIANCE

List three things you would like to expand in your life.

1. _____
2. _____
3. _____

ACKNOWLEDGE YOURSELF

For each item above, acknowledge yourself for how you have already expanded in this area.

Example: I would like more time to spend with my children.

Acknowledgment: I acknowledge myself for cutting down my TV time to spend that time with my kids.

_____
_____
_____
_____
_____

CHAPTER FOUR

LIVE YOUR LEGACY NOW

We cannot change the cards we are dealt,
just how we play the hand.
~ Randy Pausch

In the last chapter, we talked about how what we focus on expands. Now, ask yourself this question, "What do I really want people to know about me when I die?" How can you display those attributes now? If you focus on them, you'll bring them about.

The first thing that comes to mind when we hear the word "legacy" is stories of individuals and famous people such as Robin Hood, Jesse James, and Bonnie and Clyde. We also think of those who have made great contributions to the world such as Albert Einstein, Thomas Edison, and Benjamin Franklin. The word "legacy" often brings notoriety after death.

Author Barbara Greenspan Shaiman encourages people to do what her book title says: *Live Your Legacy Now.* Her message is a reminder that we do not have to wait until we die to leave a legacy. We can live our lives and create a presence fueled by passion and purpose.

Tony Robbins, the well known "in your face" coach and master of lasting change, says, "Your story is not where you came from but what you do with it from this point on."[1] You have the opportunity to create your legacy and to live the life you feel is in alignment with who you are. You can do the things you want to do to contribute positively to your community and society as a whole. You can decide to live your legacy now rather than let a legacy be created by circumstances that run your life and dictate your future.

THE LAST LECTURE

Randy Pausch wrote his bestselling book *The Last Lecture* for his children. It was based on a lecture he was asked to give after he was diagnosed with terminal cancer. Pausch, a computer science professor at Carnegie Mellon University, decided he wanted to leave something for his kids, who were young at the time, to remember him by. He didn't want to leave them only with the memory that he died of cancer.

Pausch decided to name his lecture "The Last Lecture." Instead of focusing his lecture on cancer and dying, he focused it on living. In the lecture, he demonstrated how fit he was at the time, displayed his humor, was motivating and inspiring. The messages he shared were about achieving your childhood dreams, overcoming obstacles, and helping others to achieve their dreams.

Pausch's video and book touched millions of lives because the powerful message he shared about "living" resonated with those who were putting aside their dreams. In the final moments of his lecture, he shared that his presentation was not for the audience but for his children.

---

1 *Breakthrough.* Television series. NBC. Aired July 27 and August 3, 2010.

IS THERE EVER GOING TO BE ENOUGH MONEY OR TIME TO LIVE THE LIFE THAT IS IMPORTANT TO YOU?

Living your legacy is not about living the high life, reaching materialistic goals, or being foolish and mismanaging your affairs. It is about living a life of meaning and purpose. Our daily lives, circumstances, relationships, and other events often distract us from living a life of passion and purpose. Even if you are in a relationship or have a family, you need to bring 100 percent of who you are into the mix toward creating a meaningful life. Anything less than 100 percent takes away from the vibrant potential.

Passion and purpose allow us to do things that have positive impacts on the world. Living our legacy also means living in the moment, embracing what is, and finding ways to move forward through obstacles. It means finding all the reasons why you CAN live with passion and follow through on your purpose.

You may want your legacy to be remembered as an inspiring parent, a loving member of the community, someone who is generous with his or her time, an advocate for finding homes for homeless children, or someone who stands up for civil rights. Living through passion, purpose, and integrity allows you to contribute to the world with a higher consciousness.

Whatever you want your legacy to be, take a look at your life now and see how congruent it is with where you would like it to be. Ask yourself the following questions and write down the answers. Writing them down helps you become clear on what you want.

WHAT WOULD I LIKE TO LEAVE AS MY LEGACY IN THIS LIFETIME?

_____

_____

_____

_____

_____

_____

_____

_____

_____

On a scale of 1-10, 1 being living my legacy 10 percent of the time and 10 being living my legacy 100 percent of the time, where would you rate yourself? _____

Ask three people, "If I died today and you were to say three things about me that stand out in your mind at my funeral, what would you say?"

Person #1:

   1. _____

   2. _____

   3. _____

Person #2:

   1. _____

   2. _____

   3. _____

Person #3:

1. _____

2. _____

3. _____

Now, compare what they said and make notes on the similarities, differences, and what you did or didn't like about their responses. **Be cautious here!** This exercise is not about pleasing others. It is about seeing whether or not your voice is being heard, translated, or communicated in a manner that resonates with who you are and what you believe to be true about yourself. Shift through any patronizing remarks and look for the real value.

Notes to myself:

_____

_____

_____

_____

_____

_____

_____

_____

_____

_____

_____

_____

_____

_____

Living your legacy now is really about supporting you on your path as we discussed in Chapter 1: Vision. Now is a great time to make adjustments to fulfill your "stamp of approval" on your own life. It doesn't matter how old you are, your current situation, or where you are in life. What matters is that you are being the best you can be. Being the best you can be is perfect for making a positive difference in this world.

In 1991, I started working for a construction material supplier. It was a family owned business, started by a man named Don Deer; the business grew from its humble beginnings into a multi-million dollar business. Don pioneered many new products, systems, and formulas for the construction industry.

At the time, I was the sales and marketing manager. Part of my job was to increase the market share, get to know potential customers better, and increase business with the existing customers. One day as I was walking into a restaurant with a customer, a stranger jumped up and came over to me, stopping me in my tracks. He had seen the company logo embroidered on my shirt, so he wanted to tell me what a great company I was working for, and how if it weren't for Don Deer, he wouldn't be in business. He said that Don had given him a chance, believed in him, given him credit, and supported him through the tough times. This occasion was just one of many times when I was approached about Don's generosity and kindness. As I reflect back, I realize maybe the company was a vehicle for Don to make a difference by helping others in this world.

Don was succeeded by his son, Jeff, who was much like his dad. Jeff was intelligent, personable, and genuinely cared about people. One of the things that impressed me about Jeff was that he tried to keep as many people employed as he could through tough economic times.

I remember interviewing with Jeff in early 1991, sitting across from his desk on a leather chair. As we were bringing the conversation to a close, he asked me whether I had any questions or anything else that I wanted to share. I asked him to give me a chance to show him what I could do. Ten years later, I was his vice president and general manager before moving on to my next venture. Jeff continues his dad's legacy, and he also started to create his own through his visionary and innovative leadership qualities.

SMALL STEPS, BIG IMPACT

Not everything we strive for represents a grandiose platform. We are led to believe that megastars, talk show hosts, and those in the spotlight are the great contributors to the world. Contrary to that belief, everyone is significant and unique and brings something special to the world every day.

The collective power of the grass roots movements in all countries is what will help to change this world for the better. Every day that we live our legacies, we become more connected to lives of passion, purpose, and fulfillment.

When Richard "Dick" Proenneke retired, he decided to live in a place of peace and solitude. He built a cabin on Twin Lake in Alaska and lived alone for thirty years. He cut the trees for his cabin, let the wood age, and slowly built his cabin. Everything was handmade, and it was fascinating to watch him carve out a spoon from a piece of wood, something I bought from a store and took for granted.

Dick hunted, fished, and grew vegetables for his food, and he also had food flown in to supplement his meals. He fabricated his doors and created an underground refrigerator to store his food. He lived an eco-friendly, mostly self-sufficient life that he enjoyed.

Dick never set out to be in a movie or to have Sam Keith write the book *One Man's Wilderness: An Alaskan Odyssey* about him. Dick just wanted to live the life he had imagined, and in doing so, he built and lived his legacy. When Keith's book won the National Outdoor Book Award in 1999, and it was turned into the PBS hit film *Alone in the Wilderness* in 2005, it brought Dick a great deal of attention he had never expected, and it provided him with a legacy to leave others.

When you follow your passion and purpose in life, you automatically build your legacy without effort. In that pursuit, you inspire others along the way. You become the catalyst for others to recognize their brilliance, to live with passion and purpose, and simultaneously, to build their legacies. When Dick died in 2003, he left his cabin to the National Park Service. Today, the cabin is a tourist attraction, and Dick's legacy lives on through the cabin, the book, film, and the inspiration he gave millions.

OBSTACLES AND PERSISTENCE

Nothing in this world can take the place of persistence.
Talent will not; nothing is more common than unsuccessful
people with talent. Genius will not; unrewarded genius is almost
a proverb. Education will not; the world is full of educated
derelicts. Persistence and determination alone are omnipotent.
The slogan 'press on' has solved and always will solve the
problems of the human race.
~ Calvin Coolidge

As we move through business and life, we come across bumps in the road and sometimes get discouraged and frustrated. Some people give up or put their hopes, dreams, passions, and purpose on the side because it's easier. Imagine if Abraham Lincoln, Henry Ford, Walt Disney, Milton Hershey, H.J. Heinz, and P.T. Barnum had not been persistent but gave up? They would have let bankruptcy define who they were. Instead, they kept on perfecting what they did and were persistent in moving forward. Today their legacies speak for themselves.

SUMMARY

The culmination of your desires, passions, and gifts unite with the needs of this world when you allow yourself to be vulnerable and live without fear. This is the time to recognize your brilliance and own it!

Living your legacy now embraces loving yourself and giving others the permission to do the same. In doing so, you begin to connect on deeper levels that resonate with the Oneness that we all share, regardless of race, faith, background, age, or any trait that may be perceived as being different.

There is power in letting go of but honoring your past, and of being mindful of the future without letting it induce fear. Living in the present is your natural state of being. In this state, you are inspirational, motivational, and pure genius. Your ability to influence this world positively is phenomenal. Live your legacy now!

SECTION TWO

★

CONNECTION

★

Our ancient experience confirms at every point that everything is linked together, everything is inseparable.
~ Dalai Lama XIV

CHAPTER FIVE

YOU ARE THE SOURCE

You must accept the truth from whatever source it comes.
~ Maimonides

Imagine having your own grocery store right at your house. This store is stocked with your favorite foods—packaged, fresh, canned, frozen…however you like it. It also has custom meals waiting for you to place your order. This store would be your dream food resource. Can you imagine what a convenience it would be? Can you sense the excitement every time you walk into this store? Everything you walk by would bring a smile to your face because everything you ever wanted is there. To top it off, imagine that it is free! Yes, free! You have an unlimited supply forever.

You have a store, right now, that has an endless supply. You can create it, design it, and use it 24/7. This store has the ability to bring you not only your food, but also your shelter, life partner, and abundance in all forms, including love, happiness, fun, and all the good things in life. The store is You! You create the store by your thoughts and actions.

Everyone has the ability to create what he or she wants, but few use it. Systematically, from the time we start school, our environment doesn't support or encourage us to manifest from our source within. Television, movies, and the media all teach us it is easier to blame others for what we lack than to create what we need; the result is we find excuses to be unhappy rather than to succeed or live our best lives. The great news is that you can change that. Your powerful source, your fountain of creation, is still in you, and it never left.

If you have children or know someone who has children, you know that nothing but encouragement is used when a child is trying to walk or speak. You never hear the parents or anyone else say, "That's not the way you walk" when the child falls. When the child mutters, "Maaa" or "Dudda," you never say, "That's not the way you pronounce 'Mom' and 'Dad.'" People feel nothing but joy that their children have taken their first steps or said their first words.

SUPERHEROES

As a child, nothing felt insurmountable. You could be a superhero or anything you wanted. You could create forts out of sheets and cardboard boxes. You could make up friends. Your imagination made the possibilities endless. You were the source! But somewhere along the way, all that changed. The encouragement of possibilities changed to criticism, and people became cynical about other people.

We have a choice. We can create our circumstances or let our circumstances dictate our lives. Our perception creates our reality. The physical environment may not change, but how we view the situation creates a whole new world. When we become critical of ourselves, or we listen to other people's criticism, it's like we are throwing kryptonite at Superman. We are denying the superhero within us, the superhero that can create and save us from mediocrity, if we only let him or her.

AN AHA MOMENT

In 1999, I was traveling to Phoenix, Arizona on business for six weeks at a time. My wife and I were apart during most of these trips so I decided to surprise her on a return trip. I booked a weekend getaway at a place on the east side of the island of Hawaii. The pictures online of the place looked good and the rate was $155.00 night for a bungalow type cottage. I thought that for that price, it would be a nice getaway.

The weekend of our mini-retreat, my wife and I headed out toward the east side, looking for our hotel. It was at a fairly remote place, so we excitedly traversed the back roads in search of our destination. I had been expecting a resort type atmosphere tucked away in a jungle. As we approached what looked like the entrance, however, it quickly became clear that my visions of relaxing were going to be uprooted. After we checked in, I had one last hope—that the room would be nice. For $155.00, I was expecting a Sheraton type atmosphere.

Not! Instead we walked into a screened plywood box with a shower where the water went on the floor. My cell phone could not get a signal and there was no Internet connection. "What kind of place is this?" I thought to myself. To top it off, they served only vegetarian food.

I was totally frustrated and miserable! For about half a day, I whined and complained. Then, I gave in. I decided to embrace what was and not fight it anymore (I really had no choice). As my tension began to dissolve, I realized how much I had been out of touch with myself and what really matters in life. The transition was that quick. I had been leading such a fast-paced life that I had forgotten what it was like to breathe! In that moment, I had the realization of what is truly life, the connection that Nature has to Spirit. My corporate ego dissolved as I bolted toward reconnecting with the long lost friend I had missed for so long and didn't even realize—myself. I wasn't about to lose this friendship again, so I knew life as I knew it would have to change. I did not know, how, when, or where, but I knew that my life would be different.

NOT AGAIN!

Have you ever wondered why we have the same situations repeat themselves? Whether it is the type of people we attract into our lives, the same financial situation, or any other repetitive situation that doesn't resonate with us, we must learn the lesson that it brings or it will occur over and over again.

> *Insanity: doing the same thing over and over*
> *again and expecting different results.*
> *~ Albert Einstein*

It is often said that if those who cannot handle their finances properly win a million dollars, within a year or two, they will lose it all. BankRate.com featured an article about eight lottery winners who lost all their winnings. Although a variety of reasons existed for their losses, not changing how they handled their money became their primary downfall. Evelyn Adams was a two-time winner of the New Jersey Lottery, totaling $5.4

million. Today she lives in a trailer and is broke.[1] By continuing to use the same patterns of money management and beliefs around money, her winnings quickly dwindled, leaving her in the same situation prior to her winnings.

THE CORE

You are the Source! When you realize you are inseparable from your Source of Divine Presence, you can master your ability to realize an infinite supply of abundance in every size, shape, and form. Abundance can be in many forms, including energy, love, happiness, and prosperity. With this realization, you can move forward with knowing that what you radiate outward is what you receive back. For example, if you have a mindset of scarcity or lack, then you will always not have enough. Can you think of anyone who fits this description? Do you know people who always describe others' lives as being filled with drama, but really, that is also an accurate description of their lives? As we say in coaching, "If you spot it, you got it!"

A major difference exists between the knowing and the being in this concept. In the knowing, intellectually we know how it should be, what is right, and what makes sense, but the ego mind prevents us from taking action and embracing the concept that we create our own realities. The ego wants to blame, so there is no self-reflection of responsibility. Blaming others is a false protection method that creates a barrier to the connection of the ultimate truth—our real source of power and inspiration—your Source of Divine Presence and you. In Chapter 15, we will explore more about the ego.

---

1 Goodstein, Ellen. "Unlucky lottery winners who lost their money." http://www.bankrate.com/brm/news/advice/20041108a1.asp. Accessed April 21, 2011.

MAN'S SEARCH FOR MEANING

In his groundbreaking book *Man's Search for Meaning*, Viktor Frankl chronicled his life at a concentration camp during World War II. He concluded that everything in life has meaning, even suffering. Finding meaning was the key to survival.

During his stay, Frankl observed why some people survived and others didn't when everyone ate the same food and was treated equally. The difference was the realization of the freedom of choice and faith in the future, even while suffering.

Freedom of choice and faith in the future are both derived from within. The realization Frankl had was that he was the source of his choice and he had the power to survive right there within him. That knowledge was his secret over his captors. As a result, he was able to survive and tell his story.

A CHOICE

You can choose right now to realize that you can have the life you desire, regardless of your current situation, and that it all starts with you. That choice and the results all begin with the thoughts you choose to think.

A great deal of research has been done on the mind-body connection and how our thoughts can alter our physical being. Previously discussed in theory, the mind-body connection is now being backed up by science to prove what many of us already knew—our thoughts control our reality.

Louise L. Hay, author of *You Can Heal Your Life*, has helped thousands of people to use their creative powers for personal growth and self-healing. Her own experiences of sexual and physical abuse led her to discover the self-destructive patterns they had caused on her thoughts, and by extension, her body and her health. Later, these patterns revealed themselves in the form of cancer. Without any money, Hay was told by her doctors that they would not treat her, and they estimated she had only six months left to live.

But something within Hay told her to listen carefully to the religious sermons she had been attending. They sparked within her the desire to start doing research about health and patterns of abuse. With the help of a therapist, she was able to move past her anger and resentment. Simultaneously, she searched for all the healing information she could find. She worked on cleansing her physical body as well as her emotional state of mind.

Hay was able to transform her thoughts from anger and resentment to thoughts of love. A neglected physical body changed to a body temple. With the help of a nutritionist, she was able to cleanse and detoxify her body. Six months later, there was no trace of her cancer.

Hay could easily have given up and continued to blame her abusers and succumb to her own death. Instead, she was able to realize that she was the ultimate Source and connected to the Divine Presence; her power and that connection would not only help her, but they would also help her to change the world.

Hay has gone on to help people worldwide with books and tapes and by establishing Hay House, a publishing company for self-help books. Louise Hay's incredible impact upon the world has provided healing to millions of people, all the result of her realization that she had the power to change her situation because she was the Source of her own well-being!

REFLECTIONS OF YOU

You look in the mirror every day—some of us even look in the mirror multiple times a day—to make sure everything looks good. However, one thing you cannot do is stand in front of a mirror and not see yourself. Sounds funny? Try it some time! If you are able to stand in front of the mirror and not see yourself, I will send you a free copy of this book for you to give to a friend. (Your friend is going to have to wait a long, long time.)

Just like your reflection in the mirror, you cannot escape that your thoughts and actions reflect back upon you and influence your future. The advantage to this fact is that it gives us the option to create what we really want. This option does not discount the realities of what you may have been through or what you are presently going through; however, it is the all prevailing truth that you have everything within you now to make a difference in your life and in the lives of others.

SITUATIONAL DOUBT

Sometimes our situation creates doubt. When doubt is present, fear takes over and our ability to see that we are the ones who create our circumstances is marred by an imposter. The imposter parades around, gathering all the reasons and excuses for why we are where we are. At these times, our ego gets in the way, focusing on our fears, including our fear of success, making us doubtful of our own power as the Source that can create what we want.

THE SECRET

The film *The Secret* brought much attention to the Laws of Attraction and Manifestation. The movie's main theme is the premise that we are the Source. You can create an intention through your thoughts and have those thoughts materialize.

Why was the movie so popular? I believe its popularity was for two reasons. First, people were looking for alternative answers to where their lives were headed, how to have a meaningful life, and how they could get there. The film resonated with people on a high vibrational level. The freedom felt by the baby boomers and popularized by the era of Woodstock had disappeared in the succeeding decades, but now, people wanted that sense of freedom back. They wanted to feel free rather than strapped to a high mortgage, a job that had no meaning, or relationships that served no purpose. They wanted to be happy.

The second reason for the film's popularity was that it created doubt. It challenged the viewers' core beliefs about how to achieve the ideological definition of success. It also challenged how people's Source of Divine Presence was integrated into their lives. Most importantly, it opened their minds up to the possibility that they have the power to create their own lives rather than to accept what they have. The movie gave viewers the permission to tap into their greatness and not fear what they had always sensed. The movie provided an environment in the mind that was conducive to our greatness thriving.

IT STARTS WITH A THOUGHT.

Within the seed lies the dream of a tree.
~ Jeff Bow

Our thoughts and ideas are the seeds of greatness. Imagine the power of our thoughts. While recognizing that you are the Source, think about some of the things you say daily. What you are saying about traffic, other people, yourself, your job, or other areas of your life?

Look at the words below and take the time to jot down any thoughts that come to your mind immediately. Do not "try" to think of something to write; write down what comes to mind immediately.

Traffic:

_____

_____

_____

Your relationships:

_____

_____

_____

Your job:

_____

_____

_____

Other people:

_____

_____

_____

Yourself:

_____

_____

_____

Other areas:

_____

_____

_____

How do your thoughts serve you at this moment? If you were broadcasting seeds for your future, what would you manifest in the future based on your thoughts? With every thought, you are creating your future. If your thoughts are positive and inspiring, so will your future be positive and inspiring. If your thoughts are negative, so will your future be what you are thinking. We will address how to balance our thoughts in more detail in Chapter 8: Brilliance Through Balance. (But you can take a sneak peek now at the Brilliance Through Balance Wheel in Chapter 8 to do a quick analysis of your thoughts.)

Think of your thoughts as being similar to a water source. Bottled water has skyrocketed into a multi-billion dollar industry. In 2008, bottled water sales were estimated to be $11.2 billion.[2] The reason people are flocking to bottled water is because they don't like what they are getting from their sources of drinking water. If you do not like what you are getting in your life, wouldn't it be wise to look at the Source—You!

HOLDING THE KEY

During my freshman year in high school, I had a great math teacher named Mr. Peterson. He had an interesting observation about our class. He labeled us as "the advanced class that was anti-advanced." It's amazing how we, at the time, had control of our destiny but didn't know that power existed within us. Instead, we were rebels without a cause, having a great time, when all the while we were holding the key to our futures.

Non team sports such as golf and triathlons are great illustrations of how one has to draw from within to bring together the mind, body, and spirit to overcome all odds to win. Natascha Badmann, a six-time world championship winner of the Ironman Triathlon in Kailua-Kona, Hawaii, is a perfect example of how bringing together the mind, body, and spirit makes us powerful.

I had the pleasure to watch Badmann win the Ironman. What I found incredible was that when she was within two miles of the finish line, she started waving and smiling, and she looked as fresh as she did when she started the race! Here was someone about to complete an event that consisted of swimming 2.4 miles, biking 112 miles, and running 26.2 miles!

Afterwards, during an interview, Badmann was asked how she was able to look so fresh and happy toward the end. She com-

2 Rodwan Jr., John G. "Confronting Challenges." *Bottled Water Reporter*. April/May 2009. 12-18.

mented that she felt the energy of the island and took it all in. She also said that in those last two miles, the crowd was her reward.

Badmann grew up in a less than desirable situation as a youth. She became pregnant when she was eighteen. In her twenties, she was an overweight, single parent who never exercised. Now she is an icon for other aspiring tri-athletes in the world and a role model for many men and women. She attributes a lot of her success to the power of deep believing.

SELF-RESPONSIBILITY

The world provides us with many opportunities to use as excuses for why we cannot achieve our goals, find happiness, or live the life we have always dreamed of living. Many people choose to engage in the excuse mentality so they do not have to take responsibility. The underlying sense I receive from these people is their unwillingness to acknowledge they are responsible for their lives.

We are the source for our own health and wellness, our happiness, fulfillment, our fun, and the ability to share our gifts with the world. Our gifts are the highest realization of our purpose in this lifetime and the full expression of who we are. By recognizing and honoring the gifts that others are sharing in this world, we connect all of us as One.

The power we each hold this very moment is phenomenal. We have a choice to use it or not use it. It's a choice everyone has. Let me say that again. **It's a choice everyone has!**

Make a positive difference in someone's life today! Hopefully, you will start by making such a difference in yours!

CHAPTER SIX

THE BODY-MIND-SPIRIT CONNECTION

Let's assume that each person has an equal opportunity, not to become equal, but to become different. To realize whatever unique potential of body, mind and spirit he or she possesses.
~ John Fischer

It's interesting how some phrases in life become overused. When we hear them, the tendency is to ignore what is potentially good information and possibly life-changing. "Body, mind, and spirit" is one of those "catch all phrases" used in marketing to the New Age movement and to the baby boomer generation.

In this chapter, we will be exploring how the body-mind-spirit connection is of the utmost importance in *breaking through fear and igniting your brilliance.*

The interconnection between the *body, mind, and spirit* is like a train's railroad cars linked together. When something happens to one, it affects the others. If the locomotive that drives the cars is sputtering along, then, they will all sputter along. If everything is working right and moving along, then all the cars that make up the train set run with precision.

SOUR LEMONS

If you had a lemon slice and I asked you to take a bite, what would happen? More than likely, your parotid glands would secrete saliva into your mouth. If you didn't take a bite but thought about it and placed the lemon slice in front of your mouth, what would happen? You would probably have the same reaction. Your mind knows that your body has experienced tasting a lemon before so it is reacting in preparation for a sour squirt! Now, try it again, this time imagining the lemon in front of your mouth, and think of biting into it. If you were now to try to stop your mouth from watering, the odds are that you could not stop it.

There is no separation with the *body, mind, and spirit.* They are connected as one. Therefore, what we do to one affects the other two. We may not see immediate effects or results externally, but internally, our body goes to work immediately. Think of how a disease is created. It may start with environmental pollution, pesticides in our food, smoking, or drinking.[1]

THE BODY

The physical form is a container and part of the triad of the connection—Body, Mind, and Spirit. Physically, when the

---

1 **Disclaimer:** As we move through this chapter, I will be sharing information I have personally found useful. I am not a medical doctor, nutritionist, or health professional, and I do not claim to provide any information that may cure, heal, or treat any condition. The examples provided are to illustrate the points and ideas being discussed. Always seek the advice of a certified and trained medical professional prior to starting any program that may affect your health or well-being in any way. The information provided here is not based on specific research. I encourage you to do your own research on what works best for you and to learn as much as you can to maintain optimal health.

body does not function at optimal levels, it becomes more difficult to connect with the mind and spirit and to maintain that connection.

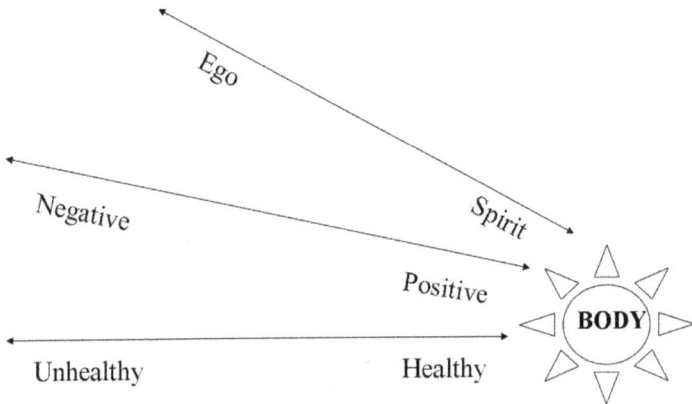

Think about a time when you were sick and lying in bed with the flu or other ailments. What did you feel like doing? Were you motivated to exercise? Did you feel like balancing your checkbook? Did you feel like meditating or going to a spiritual workshop? When we are not feeling well physically, nothing else really matters. It doesn't matter how much money is in the bank, how big and nice your house is, how many friends you have on your favorite social networking site, or what kind of car you drive. You have one motivation, which is to get well.

When I was young and carefree, I could party all night, come home at 5:00 a.m., and start work at 7:00 a.m. A hangover was there to welcome me many times. I remember saying to myself, "If I get through this, I'll never do that again..." but of course, I did.

Our body is a work of art. Yes, stop laughing! It is! It really only needs food, shelter, and water to survive. It is a phenomenal vehicle to house our mind and spirit. All we have to do is take care of it. The key to great health is maintenance and prevention.

EDUCATION

Two of the easiest ways we can maintain optimal physical health is through education and taking action. I often used to hear, "How can you have high cholesterol when you are so slim?" This statement was just an indication of how people can be confused or misinformed since high cholesterol has no relation to a person's size.

When I was younger, I was once talking to my mother about how eating a certain food was not good for me. My mother replied, "Pretty soon, if you listen to everyone saying don't eat this or that, you'll never eat anything." To a certain extent, she was right. It is no wonder we are confused with so much contradictory information. One day something is not good, and the next day, it's okay or even beneficial. Even the USDA has changed its recommendations over the years. It reminds me of what a research professor once said in a tongue-in-cheek way. He said, "Researchers are never wrong." If their research doesn't prove their theory, then they just do more research until it does.

Education comes first, but then, you have to determine what's right for your individual body. Everyone is unique and there is no other individual exactly like you in this world.

MOVE, MOVE, MOVE

Use it or lose it! Our body needs to move, approximately 10,000 steps in a day on average. The number of steps can be traced back to research done by a Japanese walking club thirty years ago.[2]

Following are pedometer (steps per day) indicators for physical activity in healthy adults measured by steps per day:

< 5,000 Sedentary Lifestyle

5,000-7,499 Low Active Lifestyle

7,500-9,999 Somewhat Active lifestyle

>10,000 Active lifestyle

> 12,500 Highly Active

Ten thousand steps is roughly equivalent to thirty minutes of exercise[3]. This number varies for children and elderly adults. It also does not take into account the intensity and terrain. These results were taken from walking (aerobic exercise) on a fairly flat surface; therefore, results may vary.

2 Tudor-Locke, C. and Dr. Bassett Jr. gHow Many Steps/Day are Enough? Preliminary Pedometer Indices for Public Health. h Department of Exercise and Wellness, Arizona State University. http://www.ncbi.nlm.nih.gov/pubmed?term=preliminary%20pedometer%20indices. Accessed April 13, 2011.

3 http://www.phs.org/americaswalking/health/health20percentboost.html. Accessed April 21, 2011.

TOP 10 REASONS FOR AEROBIC EXERCISE ACCORDING TO THE MAYO CLINIC[4]

1. Keep excess pounds at bay

2. Increase your stamina

3. Ward off viral illnesses

4. Reduce your health risks

5. Manage chronic conditions

6. Strengthen your heart

7. Keep your arteries clear

8. Boost your mood

9. Stay active and independent as you age

10. Live longer

You can go to Mayoclinic.com to find out more information on how aerobic exercise can be of benefit to you.

One of the reasons why we are seeing an increase in childhood obesity is due to the sedentary lifestyle of many youths. They are more content to be on the computer, playing video games, or watching TV than to be hiking, playing outside, or riding bicycles.

YOU ARE WHAT YOU EAT!

We all basically know what is and isn't good for us to eat. However, we usually do not focus on our health until we are sick rather than healthy. Health and fitness guru Jack LaLanne

4   http://www.mayoclinic.com/health/aerobic-exercise/EP00002/NSECTION-GROUP=2. Accessed April 18, 2011.

believed, "You are what you eat" and he lived a lifestyle that testified to that belief. Born in 1914, Jack was known for his healthy eating and physical fitness. He was an author, lecturer, nutritionist, and physical culture expert. He set many world records that displayed his endurance and physical abilities, and he won numerous awards. Jack embodied great health, well-being, and endurance. He taught about juicing fruits and vegetables in order to extract the important vitamins, nutrients, and enzymes they contained. Today, juicing has become a standard in the health food world. LaLanne's healthy lifestyle kept him inspiring people until his death in 2011 at age ninety-six.

Volumes of books have been written about how what we eat relates to our health. I believe all this information boils down to common sense, education, and moderation. The foods we were raised on aren't necessarily good for us. I was raised in Hawaii where breakfasts consisted of white rice, eggs, bacon, sausages, or Spam. Yes, Spam! Hawaii is the world leader in Spam consumption. I used to eat a pound of crispy bacon at a sitting. I did it because it tasted good. As a result, I was rewarded with high cholesterol.

A lot of people were raised during tough economic times so they were taught to use whatever was available that would minimize waste, and to eat everything on their plates because people were starving elsewhere. However, while these beliefs and teachings were well-intentioned, they have resulted in people's health being compromised, and the negative effects on their health not being realized until later in life.

EAT LOW FAT, LOW SUGAR, HIGH COMPLEX CARBOHYDRATES AND HIGH FIBER

Dr. Terry Shintani, whose work was published in the June 1991 issue of the *American Journal of Clinical Nutrition* (*AJCN*), created the Wai'anae Diet Program and the Hawaii Diet. He created the Wai'anae Diet pilot program after noticing the high rates of obesity and chronic disease in Native Hawaiians. Western influences had changed the way the native Hawaiian people ate to such an extent that the once healthy population now had the worst health of any state in the nation. The population's bad health was attributed to its poor diet.

The Wai'anae Diet Program implemented a low fat, low sugar, high complex carbohydrates, and high fiber diet based on a traditional Hawaiian diet. Over twenty-one days, the average weight loss of those on the diet was seventeen pounds. Cholesterol fell 14 percent, and blood sugar and blood pressure also fell dramatically. During this study, the participants had no increase in physical activity. The same principles from the Wai'anae Diet Program can be applied to other cultures as well. In addition to those principles, I suggest:

- **Eat Fresh, Local, and Organic when possible.**
- **Better yet, eat Biodynamic-, Pesticide-, and Chemical-Free.**
- **For Meat Eaters, Free Range, Cage-Free, Natural, and Vegetarian-Fed Meat is always best.**

Whenever possible, the best resource for food is to grow your own. That way, you know what you are putting into the soil, on the plants, and what kind of environment your food is grown in.

Eating fresh fruits and vegetables, raw when possible, provides the best nutritional value. Raw foods provide much needed enzymes for digestion. Enzymes are not present in foods cooked over 115 degrees. Some foods contain high amounts of oxalic acid. Dr. Andrew Weil says cooking these foods breaks down the oxalic acid so we can benefit from other available nutrients. These include foods such as taro leaves, rhubarb, parsley, beets, Swiss chard, collard greens, radishes, and spinach since they have the highest oxalate content. Check with your doctor or nutritionist for more information and your specific needs.

When eating conventionally grown foods, use a vegetable wash that helps to remove the residue on the surface of fruits and vegetables. Peeling away the outer layers also will help to reduce your exposure to pesticides.

How ironic that I am sitting here writing this chapter at a University of Washington Medical facility while waiting for a relative who is about to undergo treatment for liver cancer. Although many theories exist for the causes of cancer, no one person or institution has a permanent solution to the absolute prevention and cure of this disease.

What has been a consensus among health professionals is that the higher the acidity of your body, the more likely your immune system will be compromised. As a result, the probability of disease manifesting itself is very high. Foods that contribute to an acidic body are red meats, cheese, dairy products, soda, and sugars.

The people of Vilcabamba, Ecuador are known for their longevity. In addition to the clean air they breathe and the naturally grown foods they eat, many believe that the highly alkaline water they drink is a significant contributor to their longevity. Today, several products on the market reproduce alkaline water.

In Kailua-Kona, Hawaii, The Ocean Technology Environmental Center (OTEC) brings up pathogen free seawater from 3,000 feet below the surface. Many other companies desalinize water and have made it commercially available.

As we discussed earlier, we are each unique. George Burns smoked cigars until he died at age one hundred. We can only do our best to maintain optimal and vibrant health with what works best for our personal make up.

Some products found in foods have been known to affect one's health adversely over time. These include: additives, preservatives, antibiotics, growth hormones, sugar, food coloring, msg, anything artificial, and pesticides. Read labels and try to avoid anything a sixth grader or you cannot pronounce.

If possible, avoid or minimize your intake of refined foods, such as those with white flour, sugar, artificial flavorings or color, partially hydrogenated oils, saturated fats, or processed foods.

Incorporate more fruits and fresh vegetables, whole grains, complex carbohydrates, and pure water into your eating and health program.

The best gift you can give to your loved ones is your well-being. Take the time to learn about proper nutrition, natural foods, and healthy environments. Be your brilliant self and let your body be the best it can be so your mind and spirit also can flourish!

THE MIND

Remember, you are the only person who thinks in your mind! You are the power and authority in your world.
~ Louise L. Hay

It is our mind that separates us from other animals. It allows us to move beyond survival with the ability to create our circumstances. We also have the ability to make choices. We can choose to be happy in every moment. We can let our Source of Divine Presence shine through us so we may inspire others to do the same.

Handle them carefully, for words have more power than atom bombs.
~ Pearl Strachan Hurd

Words are powerful symbols that affect our psyche. With affirmations, we can change our perceptions, focus on having fun, enjoy life, and be fulfilled. It's often "in vogue" to use certain vocabulary that may be read or heard in magazines, books, or in movies, but before you do so, determine how those word choices serve you. Language used in reality shows often focuses on creating drama. Imagine what effects the power of certain words would have on you.

The consistency of the words we choose to use everyday collect in our data bank, the mind. If we are consistent in our positive thoughts, our mind will assimilate those positive words as the truth. Conversely, if our thoughts are negatively based, our mind will accept that as the truth. Our mind looks for consistency. The more consistent we are, the less likely our mind will question whether or not the action or thought is a reality.

The desire not to question is one of the reasons why most people do not like change. Change breaks the fluidity of consistency. Whether it is a changing a job, a change in marital status, or moving, change is viewed as disruptive to the mind. Even if we think the changes are good, we still feel resistant. Other situations where resistance to change might occur are when someone has a new child, a new diet, introducing exercise, or even self-development. Self-development is especially an interesting area. Think about how many people you know who have read a multitude of self-help books and who give advice to everyone else, but when they are really the ones who need to change, they never take their own advice. That doesn't mean they are not well-meaning; it's just that internally, they are not willing to move forward. It's easier for the mind to make excuses and place blame than it is to take self-responsibility.

How many of us felt that we could change our partner once we were together or married? Not!

Have you ever met someone you thought was too good to be true. You thought no one could possibly be as good, positive, or optimistic as this person? Every time you met this person, he/she was consistently the same. After time passed, you accepted the fact that this person was the real deal. It also works in reverse. You can meet someone else whose integrity is questionable, and over time, find that to be true. Your mind will, at some point, conclude that this is how and who this person is. That's one of the reasons why people say, "First impressions are the best." And once we set an opinion of a person, it's hard for us to change that opinion.

WHY ARE COMPANIES WILLING TO PAY COACHES AND CONSULTANTS TO HELP NAVIGATE CHANGE?

Companies know that their teams view the members of management as biased participants during change because usually the management is the creator of the change. Having outsiders come into a company to help and interpret the change brings understanding to how the change is relevant. This process is essential in getting the teams back to a sense of normalcy and to being productive. As a result, some side benefits may be increased motivation and inspiration.

OPTIMISM IS CONTAGIOUS!

Whidbey Island Bank has a great saying, "Optimism is Contagious." It feels good to be around happy, motivational, and inspiring people. They uplift our spirits and open our minds to more possibilities. When our minds are open, positive, and optimistic, we bring out the greatest potential within. The connection to our body and spirit increases and we become more congruent to the "true nature" of who we really are.

When I was younger, I did what most testosterone-increasing young men would do: I lifted weights. It improved my body physically, made me feel good, and boosted my ego. For me, it was a one trick pony. Lifting weights helped to improve my physical body, but it did little to connect my mind and spirit.

Then I discovered yoga. At the time, I was traveling often and it was difficult to find a gym close to where I was staying. So I decided, since I had seen a thirty-minute yoga video with Rodney Yee, to try out yoga. I bought the video, tried yoga, and liked it. Rodney was one of the first to produce yoga videos and was criticized for commercializing yoga away from its true roots. His response was that if he could get more people interested and exposed to yoga through his methods and videos, then they would at least try yoga. I am a testimonial to that!

Yoga is an excellent discipline. When I first saw people doing yoga, I thought it looked easy and told myself, "I could do that easily." Little did I know that yoga would become the best integrative practice I have ever experienced. Outwardly, the goal appears to be to achieve the twisted, complicated poses. At some point it may be, but for most practitioners, what makes yoga worthwhile is the integration of the pose with your body type and the acceptance of where you are. Yoga challenges you to work with your body, letting go of the notion of competing with others or with yourself. This attractive dynamic sets yoga apart from other disciplines.

Yoga challenges you to stretch yourself physically and mentally. It invites you to go both deeper into the poses and deeper into the exploration of your spiritual oneness.

MINDFULNESS

Dr. Ellen J. Langer, a Harvard University Psychology Professor, focuses on several areas of expertise including mindfulness theory. Her work has won numerous awards and academic honors. She changed the theory that some problems are unalterable and inevitable. Instead, she made it clear that most people have their reality shaped by mindlessness through their upbringings, associations, and repetitive exposure. Through her research and work with the elderly, Dr. Langer was able to show how mindfulness can change someone from being unhealthy to healthy. She has also applied her philosophy to learning and business.

In her book *Mindfulness*, Dr. Langer stresses process over outcome. Focusing on the process opens us to new information and perspectives, and it allows us the free rein of intuition and creativity.

Eastern traditions have long connected health problems to our emotions. Traditional Chinese medicine and Ayurvedic medicine use this connection as their basis for treatment. I recall a conversation I had with my doctor regarding Chinese medicine and the use of herbs. He was a conventional M.D. of Chinese descent, but he wanted to integrate Chinese medicine into his practice. When he had questioned an herbalist about proof, research, and evidence of how and why the herbs worked, the herbalist simply replied, "It just works." At that time, little research or statistical proof existed for such practices, so he could not incorporate Chinese medicine into his board regulated practice.

Today, however, people are turning more and more to alternative treatments to heal their bodies. Once thought of as "New Age," holistic approaches are increasingly being integrated into conventional medicine. The holistic approach views the body as whole and inseparable. Therefore, both the cause and treatments are approached as being interconnected. Your mother may have been right when she said, "It's all in your head."

Our mind is such a powerful tool. Many people strive for freedom, but I believe that freedom is a state of mind. Some financially successful people, who would outwardly appear to have the freedom that others desire, may have their freedom thwarted by constant fear they will lose their wealth or never have enough. The same is true for those who don't have money. As Sir Richard Francis Burton said, "Broke is a temporary condition; poor is a state of mind."

STUFF HAPPENS

Hurricanes, tornados, drive-by shootings, tidal waves, and all sorts of events that are out of our control can be catastrophic and wreak emotional havoc upon our lives. Dr. Wayne Dyer, however, expressed the best way for us to react to such events when he spoke about the tidal wave in Thailand. He said there was nothing any of us could have done to stop it, and that continually talking about what a tragic event it was over and over again does nothing for the healing of that area and country. The best way to help the people suffering from the effects of the tidal waves was to send positive energy and healing thoughts their way.

ROCK ON

Events in our lives, both good and bad, will happen. Once something happens, we cannot change the actual event, but we have the choice either to dwell on it or to move on and not let it control us. Our minds have infinite potential. The ability to connect our body, mind, and spirit as One is a beautiful gift. No person, circumstance, or condition can alter our reality unless we allow it. Even through adversity, illness, and tragedy, there is always light. We can use the power of our mind to heal, help others, and help ourselves. The choice to do so is ours.

SPIRIT

Do you connect to your Source of Divine Presence out of convenience? Do you remember ever calling for an immediate connection with God to make a pact? I did! As a child when I got a really bad stomach ache, I would plead to God to make it go away; in exchange, I promised never to do anything bad again. Of course, that never worked. Trying to connect to your Source with expectations of an immediate outcome rarely results in your desires being manifested. A more effective way is always to be connected.

I believe the most powerful way to live is to be connected to Spirit, your Source of Divine Presence! We are all conduits to let our Divine Presence flow through us. At the core of our connection to Spirit is love.

At the opposite ends of the spectrum are Spirit and Ego. Living with a connection to Spirit allows us to see and spread love. It allows us to see and do what brings joy. It allows us all the time to be happy at any given moment. In his book *The Art of Happiness*, the Dalai Lama says that at the core of everything we do, we are striving for happiness.

One of the things I like to ask people is, "If you lost everything today, would you still be happy?" Some people allow their material possessions to define who they are; therefore, when their possessions are not there, they feel lost. Others feel that once the initial shock has subsided, they would be able to move on.

Connection to Spirit means something different to everyone. Your connection may increase when you meditate, are in nature, practice yoga, pray, chant, or live according to what you believe to be true. The more connected we are, the more we are able to see and experience unconditional love.

One time I felt closely connected to Spirit was when my wife and I camped on our seven acre property in the country for three months. We pitched a tent and lived in nature. Even the rocky ground and pouring rain could not stop us from experiencing one of the most profound times of our lives. To this day, we still talk about the value of that experience.

As we went through that experience, others frequently asked us, "Are you all right?" or "Is everything okay?" Although their questions were out of concern for our well-being, it was interesting to note that no one ever asked us whether we were having fun.

Connection to Spirit is a personal experience and journey. Through this journey, the more consistent our connection, the greater our chances of eliminating doubt, fear, and inadequacies. Eventually, we may embrace the realization that we are brilliant and possess greatness now; we are brilliant in the sense of letting our Source of Divine Presence work through us, and we are great in our capacity to influence others positively to live their passion and purpose.

NAMASTE

Namaste is the greeting commonly used in India and Nepal. Many translations and interpretations exist for this word. The most common one relates to recognizing and honoring the Spirit in the other person. In essence, you are greeting the person as a spiritual being and connecting that person's spirit to the spirit in you. What a beautiful way of greeting and living in harmony with each other.

As we look at the body, mind, and spirit integration, our ability to honor and recognize Spirit in others allows us to recognize and connect to our Spirit and Source of Divine Presence. As we discussed in Chapter 3: What We Focus on Expands, bringing your focus to this area of your life will expand the possibilities, therefore, allowing total integration with the body and mind.

SUMMARY

Our body, mind, and spirit are connected. When we consciously choose to honor the connection, we can nurture the relationship so we have greater balance in our lives. We are a powerful source of influence on ourselves and others, so the more conscious we are of the body-mind-spirit connection, the higher our vibration, and the higher our vibration, the more fluid and flowing life will be. In this state, our brilliance shines and we are unstoppable!

What commitment can you make to yourself to increase your connections to your body, mind, and spirit? Think

about what you want and write it in the corresponding categories.

The Physical Body:

_____

_____

_____

_____

_____

_____

The Mind:

_____

_____

_____

_____

_____

_____

Spirit (Your Source of Divine Presence):

_____

_____

_____

_____

_____

_____

CHAPTER SEVEN

EXTREME SELF-CARE

Health is certainly more valuable than money,
because it is by health that money is procured.
~ Samuel Johnson

Have you ever wondered what it would be like if you had some time just for you? No kids, no laundry, no yard work, no running around. It's all about you!

In this hectic world of trying to make things work, sometimes both parents are working and constantly giving. They end up giving so much that they are exhausted, not having fun, and wondering whether anyone appreciates them. Sometimes they lose who they really are in the process. Do you know who you really are?

Women in general, mothers, and especially single mothers have so much to juggle to try to make everything work. Over a period of time, they identify with their tasks rather than with themselves as unique individuals. Men are raised with the belief that they must be the breadwinners and supporters of their families. In addition, self-imposed stress to perform financially is often added pressure to make things work. Some mask this stress by saying, "I love to work." Even if this statement is true, what personal sacrifices are being made for that work?

Extreme self-care (ESC) is not just about relaxing the body; it is also about rejuvenating the mind and connecting with spirit on a level of higher consciousness. There is a lot to be said about the "being" of life rather than the "doing."

GIVING: IN THE NAME OF SERVICE

Most of our lives are spent as givers, especially if you are a mother, caregiver, service worker, teacher, trainer, in the restaurant business, or another profession that serves others. In fact, unless you do not have customers, you are in the service business.

Approximately 44 percent of your time is spent working for yourself or others on a daily basis during the work week. This is based on an eight hour day with a half hour for lunch and two hours of commute time.

Let's break down a working mother's typical day further:

1 hour prepare breakfast for family

½ hour getting kids ready for school

1 hour dropping kids off at school

1 hour drive to work

8½ hours work and lunch

1 hour drive to pick up kids and take them to after school activities

1½ hours wait until kids are finished and go home

1 hour prep dinner

½ hour dinner

½ hour clean up

1 hour sit with kids and review homework

½ hour get kids ready for bed

That's **eighteen hours** dedicated to others in a typical day, or approximately 75 percent of a typical weekday. Being a mother is actually a twenty-four hour job, so it's no wonder that mothers get burned out and need a break.

From this example, you can see how much time is dedicated to serving others. We could do the same evaluation for career men and women who are not parents but dedicate more of their time to their work or craft. In addition to their normal activities, many are volunteers who dedicate their time to worthy causes, such as supporting local schools that lack proper funding or giving time to charities that contribute to the betterment of our society and world.

As much as giving can be personally rewarding, it is about others. It is about serving others and lifting them up to receive. At some point, the givers will not be able to hold everyone up, figuratively, and they will be buried under the weight of their own goodness. The effects may creep up slowly and only reveal themselves over time as depression, low self-esteem, frustration, negativity, insomnia, bad self-image, weight gain, and other health related issues.

Giving is a great thing, but it is receiving and extreme self-care that allow you to provide a higher quality of giving. Do you remember being at the playground on a seesaw? It is a long narrow board with a seat on each end and a pivot in the middle. You sit on one side and your buddy sits on the other and you take turns pushing up with your legs. One would go up and the other would go down. You would take turns going up and down until the movement became fluid.

How would the seesaw work with just one person? It wouldn't! You can push all you want to go up, but you will just come crashing down without the counterweight of another person to balance and slow you down from crashing.

PERMISSION TO RECEIVE

It is important to give ourselves the permission to receive in the form of extreme self-care. Giving yourself permission to receive means you accept that you are worthy. Some confuse extreme self-care with selfishness. Here is the difference.

Merriam-Webster's online dictionary defines selfishness as:

1. concerned excessively or exclusively with oneself: seeking or concentrating on one's own advantage, pleasure, or well-being without regard for others.

2. arising from concern with one's own welfare or advantage in disregard of others <a selfish act>.

Selfishness is an act where there is a disregard for others.

With extreme self-care, although the focus is initially on you, it is with the intent that you cannot be the best that you can be if you don't care for yourself first. Your other roles as a parent, leader, partner, spouse, or any other role in your life will benefit in the long run from extreme self-care.

Extreme self-care may mean different things to different people. It is about doing things for you that are enjoyable such as receiving a massage, golfing, hiking in nature, or whatever helps to rejuvenate one's passion and helps to validate one's life purpose. It is recognition for all that we do and are in this world. In the process, you may also discover an increased connection with your Source of Divine Presence. It allows the process of energy to flow through us so that, in our "giving roles," we can give with the highest quality experience possible. The bottom line reason for why we should receive extreme self-care is the feeling that **"It's all worth it."** In the end, others benefit immensely from you taking care of yourself.

Some of the benefits of extreme self-care are reduced stress, renewed passion, rejuvenation, a clear mind, inspiration, validation, relaxation, motivation, a reconnected sense of self, hope, and many other possible positive outcomes. Try it; it may surprise you! Following is a request for you to rejuvenate your life. Of course, the choice is yours.

REQUEST #1

List ten ways you can rejuvenate your passion and validate your purpose.

Please remember that extreme self-care is about you. Make up the list with only you in mind, and for this exercise, do not consider what others will think etc. This is about you!

Example 1: Connecting with Nature helps you to connect to your Source. You may enjoy taking a walk on the beach, a hike, or a nature walk of some sort. "I will commit to talking a walk on the beach once a week."

Example 2: You haven't had a massage in a long time, but you know that after a massage you feel pampered, relaxed, and rejuvenated. "I will schedule an hour and a half massage for myself this week."

1. _____
2. _____
3. _____
4. _____
5. _____
6. _____
7. _____
8. _____
9. _____
10. _____

Now pick your top three extreme self-care activities above, and <u>in order of importance</u>, write them below.

Here are my top three Extreme Self-Care Activities:

1. _____

2. _____

3. _____

Write here how you would feel if you received (could participate in) these three Extreme Self-Care activities. Imagine how you will feel after you have allowed yourself to receive them:

_____

_____

_____

_____

_____

_____

_____

_____

REQUEST #2

Make a commitment to yourself. The following is a sample of a commitment to yourself to take the time you deserve now. (Please change or reword as you see fit so you are 100 percent committed.)

A letter of Understanding to Myself

I understand that in order for me to be the best I can be, I need to be able to accept the gift of extreme self-care. In doing so, I know others will greatly benefit from my ac-

tions, and I will be able to continue to be of service to others and not burn out. In the acceptance of extreme self-care, I commit to and understand the following:

- *My extreme self-care will not hurt or harm others or myself in the process.*
- *I will do the three extreme self-care items listed above or more.*
- *I will do so without guilt.*
- *I am committed to being the best I can be and to valuing who I am.*
- *I am deserving.*
- *I am committed 100 percent to making this happen; I will find ways to make this happen.*
- *I will allow myself to enjoy this experience.*
- *I will schedule this Now.*
- *I will not make excuses why it cannot be done.*
- *As a human and spiritual being, I understand the importance of taking the time to reconnect to myself and my Source of Divine Presence.*
- *I am willing.*
- *I am practicing extreme self-care because I love myself as much as I love others.*
- *I accept this extreme self-care request with full responsibility, and I hold myself accountable to complete it.*

_____   _____

Signature   *Date*

MIND BREAK – BEING IN THE NOW

Extreme self-care switches from fulfilling the needs of others to fulfilling your own needs. As a "giver," you are constantly fulfilling the needs of others. You may be fulfilling the need of hunger by cooking, the need of clean clothes, solving your employees' problems, fulfilling the needs of your spouse or partner, fulfilling the needs of your customers, or simply fulfilling a need to be heard by listening to others complain.

In 2003, my wife and I decided to take two months to travel. Two years prior to that, we had made a decision that I would leave the company where I had worked for ten years and where I had worked my way up to vice-president and general manager. At that time, we were in the middle of building a house and had no other sources of income. My boss and I worked out a severance package. It was able to sustain us for a time, but eventually, the house far exceeded our projected budget. We were stressed! We had not taken any significant time off in ten years!

Assessing our situation, we made the decision to sell what was our dream house at the time. Once we made the decision, the house sold quickly and we were able to pay off our debts and move forward. In this case, both of our extreme self-care needs were the same. We had no idea what the world would bring as far as work, but we knew it was something we needed to do.

We then shipped our van to Oakland, California, and for two months, we drove up the West Coast through California, Oregon, and Washington. We drove as far as Salt Spring Island in Canada, and then we headed back down the coast again.

We reconnected with each other, connected with those we met, and embraced the openness that life had to offer. It was the most amazing extreme self-care I have ever experienced. The value of this experience was and still is priceless.

Throughout this experience, a comment we heard from others was "I could never do that." They believed it wasn't possible for them to take time off for themselves like we were during. Our reply was, "You can; you just have to make it a priority for yourself." In the end, our actions inspired our friends to look at their lives and take the time to receive the gift of extreme self-care.

Extreme self-care is not a luxury, and it doesn't need to cost a lot of money. Plenty of things you can do right now are within your budget if you look for them. You just need to make extreme self-care a priority in your life, to understand it is something essential to help you to be the best you can be.

FLIGHT SAFETY INSTRUCTIONS

> *In the event that the oxygen level in the main cabin becomes unstable, oxygen masks will drop in front of every passenger. Passengers are to take them, secure them to their heads using the elastic band, and breathe through the masks normally. Passengers are instructed to make sure their masks are on first before assisting other passengers or children.*

These instructions are a fantastic metaphor for you to remember to give yourself extreme self-care. Putting yourself first allows you to assist others better in your capacity as a giver.

★ CHAPTER EIGHT ★

BRILLIANCE THROUGH BALANCE™

Balance. The Ultimate Goal.

~ Ricky Lankford

Do the following statements sound familiar?

1. "Where did all the time go?"

2. "There's not enough time in the day!"

3. "I need to spend more time..."

4. "I wish I had time to..."

You are already brilliant in your own right. You have skills, talents, and gifts that are unique. In this chapter, we will look at how being balanced can take your brilliance to the next level. Think about how you would balance the following areas of your life: Profession, Primary Relationship, Relationships, Self-Development, Extreme Self-Care, Spirituality, Finances, Physical Surroundings, Rest and Relaxation. Let's take a look at the average person's day.

Total Hours in a Day	24
Breakfast	.5
Commute	1
Work	8
Lunch	.5
Commute	1
Dinner	1
TV/Read/Other	1
Sleep	8
Total:	21
Remainder	3 hours

If you work ten to twelve hours a day or have a longer commute, then your three hours left shrink to almost nothing. Also, parents who have to pick up kids and go to after school activities have to factor in these times as well. How do you factor in the other categories (listed above) into your life? It's no wonder we live in a stressed out world.

Mathematically trying to balance our lives is impossible. Instead, we will explore how best to use your time based upon what is of the utmost importance to you.

Take the time to list activities in your typical day.

Activity

Amount of Time

_____   _____

_____   _____

_____   _____

_____   _____

_____   _____

_____   _____

_____   _____

_____   _____

_____   _____

_____   _____

_____   _____

_____   _____

_____   _____

_____   _____

Total amount of time   _____

Hours Left (24 minus Total)   _____

COMMITMENT TO SELF!

Finding balance starts with putting yourself first. It's difficult for some people to make themselves a priority because they have been taught to view doing so as being selfish. On the contrary, as you learned in the previous chapter on Extreme Self-Care, putting yourself first is the best thing you can do for yourself and others.

GIVING – THE FEEL GOOD EXERCISE

By nature, most of us are givers. We give our time, money, and resources to others in efforts to keep the peace, help others in need, support charitable organizations, or to ensure that our children will have better lives. These things are all good, but too much of anything can be detrimental to our well-being. We could burn out.

For example, if you gave away 100 percent of all the money you made, how could you support your family, pay the bills, and save for the future? Where would the money come from to take vacations? While this example may be extreme, it's easy to see how it would not serve you if you followed that route.

What about your time, energy, and focus? We often give of our time—sometimes a lot. Think about how the majority of your time is dedicated to your professional life. How much energy is left for other areas of your life on a daily basis? How does that serve you?

BALANCE

The definition of what is balance varies for each individual. I personally like the definition from Merriam-Webster.com: "to bring into harmony or proportion."

When a washing machine is out of balance, it makes a loud noise that can be heard from a distance. If it goes unchecked, the machine usually stops to prevent damage. We, on the other hand, do not have the same warning alarm. Our signals are usually subtle and reflective of our journeys as we veer off course.

WHERE DID I PUT MY BALANCE?

It is easy to get so caught up in our day-to-day routine that we don't even notice we are slowly losing sight of areas in our lives that really need our attention. It's funny how others notice how imbalanced we are while we remain oblivious. Even if we do notice, our motivation for change is littered with wonderful excuses of "why" to justify and maintain such a lifestyle. At other times, we are reminded that we must sacrifice ourselves for others. I have been a testimony to all these excuses.

OH NO, NOT ME!

I loved to work. Not only did I love to work, but I strived to be the best in my career and to help the company I worked for to be the best in its industry. While the effects culminated over a ten year period, the collaboration of those effects hit me one day as if I were blindsided by a freight train. I wondered what had happened and where the train had come from, but all along, my feet were firmly planted on the tracks to the destination I was headed for all along—divorce.

Logically, I knew what a balanced life should look like, but the desire and work to obtain my professional goals became stronger than I could have imagined. I had put blinders on, thinking it was my job as a man to provide. My way of providing was to work and work hard. So I did.

Even after I was divorced, I plowed further into my work to avoid confrontation with the acceptance of the truth—I had lost the game in life that really mattered.

Could I have avoided the crash? Nothing in life is certain. However, if I had known "awareness" of how balance really affected my life, I could have altered the course and focused on what was really important. I could have found a way to create a tapestry that integrated all the areas of my life. The crash may have been avoided!

CREATING A LIFE OF BALANCE: THE FOUNDATION

The place to start in bringing balance to your life is to create a baseline. From this baseline, you can determine how you would like to move forward in your life.

The following chart represents different areas of your life. Change any area that doesn't resonate with you and rename it to one that does. It is important that Spirituality (or however you define your Source of Divine Presence) remain in the center. It is humbling to know that a Source greater than ourselves connects us at the core of everything we are and we do in our lives.

Begin by filling in each section with a number from 0-10, 0 being the lowest and 10 representing the highest level of satisfaction. Write the number in the appropriate section of the Brilliance Through Balance Wheel™. The following is a brief description of each category. Again, if there is something you would like to change, please change it. This process is meant to support you in your journey.

The check-in-questions are designed to bring awareness to your thoughts that may then help trigger an accurate response.

Finances

Your current satisfaction with your financial situation.
Check in question: Are you happy for those people who are really wealthy?

Physical Well-Being

Your level of physical and emotional fitness.
Check in question: How is your self-image?

Primary Relationship

Your happiness with your significant other or being alone.
Check in question: Do I bring 100 percent of who I am to the relationship?

Relationships

Degree of happiness with others in your life.
Check in question: Are my relationships supportive or destructive?

Personal Development   Your process to be the best you can be.
Check in Question: What inspires you?

Physical Surroundings   The place you call home, workplace or state.
Check in question: Do these areas really resonate with you and support you to be the best you can be.

Rest and Relaxation   The time you allot for yourself to replenish your energy.
Check in question: When was the last time you had fun?

Profession   The level of happiness in your life's work.
Check in question: Am I doing something I love?

Spirituality   The quality of connection to your source of Divine Presence.
Check in question: To what degree do I have faith and trust in a Source greater than myself?

SAMPLE WHEEL

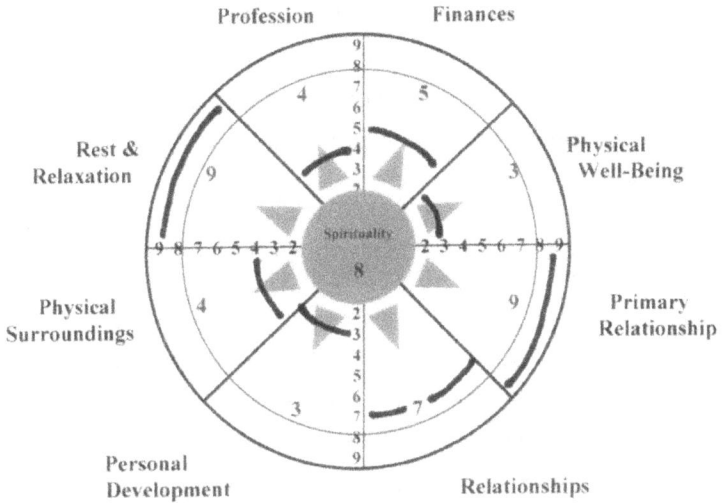

YOUR BRILLIANCE THROUGH BALANCE WHEEL™

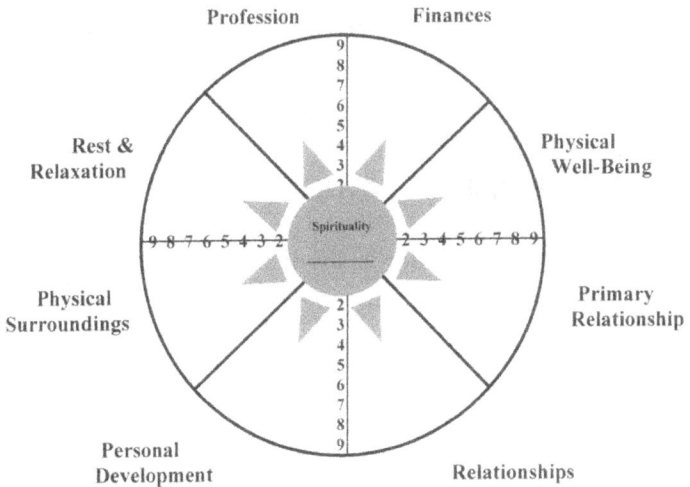

AN 8 IS AN 8—NOT!

Everyone has different life experiences; therefore, someone else's perception may be different than yours on a specific topic. Your rating of an 8 and someone else's rating of an 8 may have a different meaning and interpretation.

When you go through this exercise, it is important to do it by yourself and resist the tendency to ask someone else, "What do you think?"

NOW WHAT?

Now that you have completed the wheel, take a look at the lines and see how your wheel would roll if you were to roll it on a flat surface. Notice the areas that may need some attention.

Think about a juggler. In essence, we are all jugglers trying to balance the different parts of our lives while wanting to have fun doing it. Jugglers usually try to use objects that are of equal size and weight so it's easier to create a rhythm as they juggle. This goal holds true for you as you intertwine the different areas of your life and express your Brilliance through Balance.

WHAT IS BRILLIANCE THROUGH BALANCE?

Brilliance through Balance is about being the best in all areas of your life and not just one area. Your brilliance shines and comes forward when there are no areas in your life that weigh you down or keep your mind from exploring the world's infinite possibilities.

For example, have you ever had financial problems? Are you short of money for the bills, rent, or the mortgage? With financial problems on your mind, what percentage would you say you were focused on work when you are at work? Imagine if all of a sudden, your financial issues went away or were solved for you and you were not behind on any bills? How would you be able to perform at your job? Would you be more inspired?

Balance doesn't make the problems or obstacles in your life go away. Instead, it brings out your ability to make great decisions on how to move forward and look at solutions from an optimistic point of view. It helps you to make better choices.

Have you heard employers tell their employees to leave their personal problems at home when they come to work? That is easier said than done and places an impossible request on the employee. Let me illustrate the point in this example: Imagine having a headache. You call your boss and say you won't be coming in. Your boss tells you that your headache is a personal problem so you need to come to work. At this point, could you separate your headache from you? Sounds absurd, doesn't it?

The same holds true if you have a fight with your significant other, a death in the family occurs, or you have financial or any other problems. Separating your issues from who you are is impossible. As much as you can pretend not to let your issues affect you, they do. In order for the problem to go away, you need to deal with it.

By dealing with problems directly and finding solutions to move forward, you will bring balance back into perspective. Having balance will minimize the tendency to spread and distract others with your issues at work or at home.

Many business owners who recognize this human element in their employees and the need to balance work and personal lives have created programs to support their staff; such progressive leaders continue to make a positive difference with the people who work for them and the world.

CAN YOU STRIVE TO BE THE BEST PROFESSIONALLY AND STILL HAVE BALANCE?

If you are a working professional, the majority of your time allocation is already dedicated to your profession. Here's how you can strive to better yourself at work and provide for your family.

Negotiate it. Discuss with others who will be affected, your goals, dreams, and how achieving them will also impact their lives. Discuss how you will balance your time with them and with work. Agree on an approximate timeframe needed for you to get where you want to be professionally. Take a look at whether your professional goals are ego-based or Spirit-led. Are your goals anchored by the core values of your family, partner, or significant other? Determine a timeframe to check back with others in your life to see whether you are supporting their needs?

One of the #1 lies men and women say is, "I'm okay. Nothing's wrong." Let love, intuition, and common sense help to guide you beyond what is being said. Create an environment that is conducive to everyone being able to express him- or herself fully without fear of retribution or criticism. Ask the question, "How can I be a better support for you?"

Focus. When you get home from work, it's time to dedicate 100 percent of your attention to your loved ones. Shut off the cell phone and the computer. You can do the same in other areas of your life that need attention (refer to your Brilliance Through Balance Wheel).

Invest in quality time. Be present in the physical, emotional, and Spiritual sense. Let go of work. (In other words—don't be thinking about work when your partner, child, or friend is talking to you.) Welcome the other person(s) with love, without judgment, and listen, accept, relax, and be in the moment.

There may be a tendency to create quick fixes. An example might be that you do not spend enough time with your children, so you try to make up for it by buying them toys or dangling a carrot of future promises. These quick fixes are temporary at best and really have no long-term value. Overtime, they create a false sense of reality that at some point will crumble the foundation you thought to be the basis for your success.

> *Only put off until tomorrow what you are*
> *willing to die having left undone.*
> ~ Pablo Picasso

LIFE-ALTERING EXPERIENCES BRING GREATER CLARITY TO YOUR LIFE

From a universal standpoint, life lessons keep coming to us until we get the message and learn what we are supposed to learn. Sometimes when we don't get the message, a life-altering event, situation, or experience occurs. It may be in the form of a life-threatening disease, a health issue, a car accident, divorce, loss of a job, or some major event. When this experience occurs, it usually causes people to reflect upon their lives and to realize what is really important.

You don't have to wait until you have a life-altering experience. Take a look at your life now and make the changes you need so you may experience your Brilliance.

Connect with your Brilliance

What are you willing to commit to so you can move forward in your Brilliance through Balance? Break down your answer into the smallest, most manageable steps. This process will help you to start with achievable goals that help to build confidence in knowing you can make it happen.

Finances:

_____
_____
_____
_____

Physical Well-Being:

_____
_____
_____
_____

Primary Relationship:

_____
_____
_____
_____

Other Relationships:

_____

_____

_____

_____

Personal Development:

_____

_____

_____

_____

Physical Surroundings:

_____

_____

_____

_____

Rest and Relaxation:

_____

_____

_____

_____

Profession:

_____

_____

_____

_____

Spirituality:

_____

_____

_____

_____

CONGRATULATIONS!

You have taken the first steps to moving forward in redefining with greater clarity your Brilliance through Balance. Revisit this chapter from time to time and redo this section. Doing so will allow you to take a look at your progress and see the areas of your life that have changed.

SECTION THREE

★

ACTION

★

Talk doesn't cook rice.
~ Chinese Proverb

★ CHAPTER NINE ★

FEAR

To conquer fear is the beginning of wisdom.
~ Bertrand Russell

The number one roadblock that stops us from taking action is fear. But is fear really warranted? Dictionary.com defines fear as "a distressing emotion aroused by impending danger, evil, pain, etc., whether the threat is real or imagined; the feeling or condition of being afraid."

Innate fear is an emotional response for survival. All other fears are learned or perceived. Think about some of the things you were repeatedly told while growing up and how they influenced you, such as: "Don't go outside in the dark; the boogie man is out there," "Only bad boys and girls do that," "I won't be your friend," "You're such a prude," or "You're not cool."

There are two types of fear:

1. Fear for survival and safety.

2. Fear that protects our ego.

FEAR FOR SURVIVAL AND SAFETY

Innate fear arises when our safety is threatened. In the face of danger, our protection mechanism, known as the fight or flight syndrome, causes us to move away from danger if time permits. However, because humans have the capacity to think, analyze, and be curious, our ability to survive is sometimes thwarted because we don't always follow our instincts; instead, we try to rationalize a situation. This rationalization is evident in situations such as the "battered person's syndrome" where there is threat and evidence of harm, but instead of fleeing, the person stays and tries to justify the danger.

Humans will go and check out what's happening because of curiosity. I am certainly guilty of that. When I was living in Hawaii and the Civil Service announced that a hurricane was coming, my friends and I headed for the beach to see whether the waves were getting bigger. Not the smartest thing to do—in fact, it was pretty foolish.

On the other hand, animals, by nature, do not question when they sense danger; they just run. They move away slowly, and as the level of danger increases, so does the speed at which they move in the opposite direction of the perceived danger. You would never see a deer wander over to a pride of lions out of curiosity.

Humans, in contrast, go on safari to get as close as they can to the lions, but when a tragedy strikes and the lion attacks someone, people are "shocked" that it could happen…hmm.

When I was a boy, a rumor existed that a witch lived in the mountains. My brother, sister, and friends would talk about how scary she was and wondered what she looked like. We were afraid but curious. Even as children, no one wanted to say he or she was afraid. So instead of staying away, we set out to look for the witch in the mountains; of course, we never found her. That was probably a good thing since, if she were real, we would have been walking into harm's way.

WHAT WERE YOU THINKING?

Dateline NBC recently did a study to determine how the need to fit in outweighs our innate sense of fear for survival. The title of the program was, "What Were You thinking?"[1] Following are two of the experiments they did:

Experiment 1:

All the *Dateline* staff was in a room where a temp person was brought in for clerical work. A vapor, resembling smoke, was released and slowly infiltrated the room. The vapor was harmless, unbeknown to the temporary worker. Everyone sat around a table as the smoke continued to fill the room, to the point where they could hardly see. The *Dateline* employees just continued working because they were in on the experiment. The temporary worker just continued to work. When the show host stepped in to ask the temporary worker why he didn't say or do something, his response was that it didn't seem to bother anyone else so he kept on working despite feeling something was wrong.

---

1 http://www.msnbc.msn.com/id/21134540/vp/35951451#35951451. Aired April 26, 2010. Accessed April 18, 2011.

Experiment 2:

The premise for this experiment was a fake reality show titled, "What a Pain." *Dateline* hired aspiring actors to see how far they would go even if they felt they were hurting someone. They were told that they would be asking people questions, and if a person got the question wrong, the aspiring actor would have to shock the person being questioned. The voltage would increase if the person continued to miss questions. The actor then had to question a *Dateline* employee and the *Dateline* employee (who was in on it) was told that it was going to hurt. The employee actually didn't feel any shock but would yell and scream as if he were being shocked. The bottom line was that the aspiring actor continued to shock the *Dateline* employee even though it made him visibly upset. When the hired actors continually turned to the person pretending to be in charge of conducting the experiment, he simply said, "Please continue." The aspiring actor then continued with the shocks even when the *Dateline* employee stopped responding, as if he had died or passed out.

When questioned after the experiment was over why they continued even when they were visibly upset by the process, the aspiring actors said that the person conducting the experiment seemed so authoritative that he made them afraid not to continue.

This experiment gives us an example of how our environment and other people create a false sense of security or a need to conform that overrides our innate sense of fear in the face of danger, as well as how our fear can keep us from doing what we know to be morally right, such as to stop hurting others when we fear being hurt ourselves.

To fear is one thing.
To let fear grab you by the tail and swing you around is another.
~ Katherine Paterson

FEAR PROTECTS THE EGO

Our needs to fit in (social conformity) and to be liked are major roadblocks to accessing our true potential. We would rather fit in and not offend anyone, even when doing so makes no sense or is even detrimental. Another *Dateline* episode illustrated this point by conducting an experiment in an elevator. The elevator was filled with *Dateline* employees who were told to turn and face the back of the elevator after someone got in. The back of the elevator had no exit and was just a solid wall. The people who entered saw what the others were doing and just followed their example. Everyone was staring at the back of the elevator wall. Although not scientific, this experiment displays the human need to conform.

The ego in the form of self-esteem, self-image, and conceit can be compared to a raw egg. It is soft on the inside with a fragile protective shell on the outside. Fear has the ability to pass through the shell, take the raw egg, stir it up, and then leave with the shell intact. Each time fear passes through the shell, the shell becomes thinner and thinner.

We allow fear to become our false sense of protection. We use fear to create a seemingly unbreakable, invisible shield around our fragile shell. Fear is the perpetrator that prevents us from accessing our brilliance. This invisible shell of fear that we create defies rejection, continuity, creativity, love, communication, and a whole litany of possibilities.

FEAR RESIDES OUTSIDE OF US

It is misleading to think that fear is something internal because we have emotional responses to fear that we actually can sense within us. Our need to control falsely embodies fear so we make it a part of us. I purposely worded this book's subtitle as "How to Break Through Fear," not "How to Break Through Your Fear." Fear is universal, but how we handle it is an individual reaction and choice.

Fear is a convenient excuse not to take action. It is masked in the form of rejection, dislike, or unflattering self-reflection. Taking ownership of fear is a voluntary control mechanism much like when children are at the stage where they do not want to share their toys. We begin to make the fear be about us when, in fact, fear lies outside of us. When we do make it about us, it then becomes a part of us and the fear becomes real. Our true nature is to be caring, loving, and giving, but fear causes us to forget that.

Doubt initiates the process of fear. Doubt becomes a mirror and voice for our internal thoughts and feelings much like the process of Applied Kinesiology. Kinesiology, based on ancient Chinese medicine, can detect muscle imbalances. Muscle testing, Applied Kinesiology, can detect internal energy blockages, nutritional deficiencies, food sensitivities, and emotions.

When was the first time you remember that fear stopped you in your tracks, but you overcame it and moved on? Take the time to think in-depth about this question. All of us at one point or another in our lives have overcome fear and lived to tell the story.

Write it down now. How I broke through fear!

_____
_____
_____
_____
_____
_____
_____
_____
_____
_____
_____
_____

For me, the first time I remember overcoming my fear was in the seventh grade. I had a teacher who used fear as a tactic to keep us in line and supposedly to help us learn. We called her Sister Hard Nose (Her name has been changed to protect the alleged mean teacher), although Sister is accurate. Her theory was that your parents sent you to school to learn and to be disciplined, so you need to be quiet and sit still. Now, I believe Sister Hard Nose had the students' best interests at heart; she just didn't realize that her methods were antiquated. Once in awhile, she would whack her wooden pointer on a desk to remind us of who ran the class. Yes, we were afraid.

At the time, she was so intimidating that the majority of the students were afraid of her. I tried to bypass that fear by getting on her good side. I looked for patterns in how she graded so I could do better and show her I was learning. I discovered that Sister Hard Nose liked a lot of flowery writing, the type of writing where you took what should be one paragraph and turned it into three pages. Because I was on a mission to win her over, whenever I wrote a paper for her, I tried to be as long winded as I could and it worked. I think my writing to meet her standards made her feel her efforts to teach were validated, and that improved her opinion of me. I had successfully transformed my fear into a solution and a means to connect with someone else for our mutual benefit.

As a result of this experience, I learned that a lesson exists in every situation, every obstacle, and every roadblock we come across in our lives. If we do not learn our lesson, the situation tends to repeats itself until we do. Do you ever find yourself asking, "Why does this keep happening to me? Why do I keep attracting the same things into my life?" A better question is to ask yourself, "What could I do differently so the results change?"

TAKING ACTION

Obviously, if you fear for your physical safety, or if others are at risk, then run or move away from the danger. Call 911 if necessary. But most of our fears tend to be largely irrational. We let fear hold us back from achieving or making positive changes in our lives. That type of fear is ego-based. The bulk of ego-based fear is the fear of failure and the fear of rejection, which prevent us from moving forward to access our brilliance.

Following are five action steps you can take to overcome your fear.

1. **Understanding the risk—looking at the best and worst that can happen.**

   Hawaii is reliant on shipping to bring in 80-90 percent of all goods. When a shipping strike is threatened, people will hoard toilet paper, rice, canned goods, and other necessities. The drama of a potential strike becomes worse than the actual strike itself. Instead of thinking about the community in general and making sure there is enough to go around, people become concerned only about themselves and what they can get. And most of the time, the issues are settled before the strikes take place, making the fear unwarranted.

   Hurricane season in Hawaii is another time where fear becomes a factor, especially when, "It's headed our way." Hurricanes can be a real threat to property, people, and communities in Hawaii. But again, there is a difference between being prepared and living in fear. Whether it is prior to a hurricane, meeting a potential client, or giving a presentation, being prepared is the smart thing to do. The fear, however, that sometimes goes along with the preparation is unnecessary. You have no control over the future if the hurricane does happen, so why dream up all the destructive possibilities that might occur. Taken to the extreme, you could be afraid of every strong wind that blew while you were on vacation in Hawaii, and that would ruin your vacation.

In every situation, whether it's a sales call, someone asking to marry you, or working toward a promotion, rather than give into fear, evaluate the real risk involved.

2. Create a challenge!

In a *Fortune* magazine interview[2], Larry Page, cofounder of Google, expressed that Sergey Brin and he almost didn't create Google because of the risk and fear of failing. When Stanford University told them to try it, and if they didn't succeed, to come back to get Ph.D.'s, that was the catalyst for them to move forward on their own.

A good strategy, if you are in sales and fear rejection, is to make rejection your goal. You're almost guaranteed success if you shoot for the largest number of rejections possible. If an average ratio of sales to rejections were 1:10, you have just changed the ration to your favor. Now your chance to succeed at your new goal is 10:1. The great benefit to this goal change is that now if you fail, you will actually gain a new customer. If you're really lousy at rejection, then your business will grow exponentially. This strategy is a fun way to approach fear—and it works!

3. Make a conscious choice!

After the initial exhilaration of an idea, new process, or inspiration, a point comes where that excitement levels off and then fear takes over. Make a conscious decision

2 Serwer, Andy. gLarry Page on How to Change the World. h May 1, 2008. http://money.cnn.com/2008/04/29/magazines/fortune/larry_page_change_the_world.fortune/. Accessed April 20, 2011.

not to take ownership of the fear. It is a choice and not a reflex.

Think of this stage as similar to the period after buying a new car, the period of time before buyer's remorse sets in. At first, you are excited and happy leading up to the purchase. Your excitement level continues to increase the day you pick up the car. You drive it home, park it in the garage, and wipe off any of the fingerprints on your new paint.

The next day, you wonder whether you made the right decision, whether you can afford it, and whether you should have used the money for the car payment to pay other bills or for the kids' tuition. Although you thoroughly weighed all the options before the purchase, that voice of doubt sets in to challenge the foundations of your decision.

At this point, you should nip your doubts in the bud and stop the train from running off track into the fear zone. You now have the choice to continue forward and **look at where you want to be, not where you are at.** This step is key.

If you have ever ridden a motorcycle, you know that wherever you look is where you will go. If you look left, you go left. If you look right, you go right. If you look ahead, you go straight. If you look down, you crash.

Review your notes from the chapters in Section One and keep heading toward your vision. Remembering your larger vision, whatever the current fearful circumstances, will keep you moving forward closer to it. If you made a vision board in Chapter 1, look at it now to revisit your inspiration.

4. Check your balance meters.

When we are out of balance, as discussed in Chapter 8, our mind begins to focus on what is not working rather than what is working. For example, if you are having money troubles and you are at work, how much of your focus will actually be upon your work? If you find you are out of balance, go back to Section 2: Connection, and Chapter 8: Brilliance through Balance, and revisit the exercises to reestablish grounding.

5. Do something, anything.

Every day, do something that works to get you closer to your vision. Some things may seem small, but they may turn into big, brilliant fires that will ignite your passion. Success with small steps builds confidence and begins to dissolve self-doubt.

As you did in the exercise portion of Chapter 1, remember to "chunk it down." I would like to emphasize the point again. Take a look at your vision and break it down into smaller components. Trying to jump from your concept to bringing into reality your ultimate vision is like trying to light the biggest log in your fireplace with a match! That is a surefire way to let disappointment and doubt set in. Let's start with the kindling. Answer this question:

What small step can I take NOW to move forward in my vision?

_____

_____

_____

_____

_____

_____

_____

Summary

If this book contains one tool that is pivotal to igniting your brilliance, it is this section on overcoming fear. It is often difficult to embrace the unknown, but it is possible. In fact, each time we break through fear, we come closer to living the truth of who we really are. This realization creates an unspoken understanding and a connection to a Source greater than us.

Your highest potential to make a positive difference in this world increases with every fear conquered. The confidence, knowledge, and faith that you bring forward after each encounter leads to greater happiness, joy, love, and fulfillment.

You are greater than the sum of your fears!

CHAPTER TEN

THE CIRCLE THEORY

*It is one thing to photograph people. It is another to make others
care about them by revealing the core of their humanness.*
~ Paul Strand

Do you remember when you were a child and you told a secret
to your friend? You may have whispered it in your friend's ear
or told him or her in private. But the secret would then travel
to others, and soon, it was no longer a secret. Whether the
secret contained good or bad information didn't matter; the
word still traveled fast, and before you knew it, everyone knew
your secret.

Now imagine using this same simple process of how quickly
words spread to improve your life, change your circumstance,
or even change the world. Although it may seem simple, the
one critical factor at the center is you. The Circle Theory is
often represented as a pebble that creates a ripple effect when
tossed in the water. Concentric circles appear and spread from
the entry point where the stone hits the water.

IT ALL STARTS WITH YOU

You are at the center or nucleus of your world, not in a selfish
way, but as a child of the Universe. You are unique! No one on
earth is a replica of you, not even close. Why not celebrate it?

Each of us brings his or her uniqueness to the world, no matter what we do—whether we are business owners, leaders, employees, partners, homemakers, or any other occupation. Each of us is special. You are special. As we were brought up through school and other learning environments, we were asked to conform to the subject matter at hand and the format created by the person in authority. Never did we attend a class that celebrated one of us as an individual. Obviously, it would not have been practical to have a class for each student, or even a teacher for each student.

Now you have an opportunity really to celebrate who you are, what you stand for, and to make a difference in this world.

THE CIRCLE THEORY'S STRUCTURE

Let's take a look at how the Circle Theory might work for a business.

The Circle Theory's structure may look like this:

Vision (Owner) & Values ⇨ Executive ⇨
Top Level Leaders ⇨ Managers ⇨ Employees

Depending on the company's structure, other layers may be in-between. Transferring this information so it fits into the Circle Theory, it would look like this:

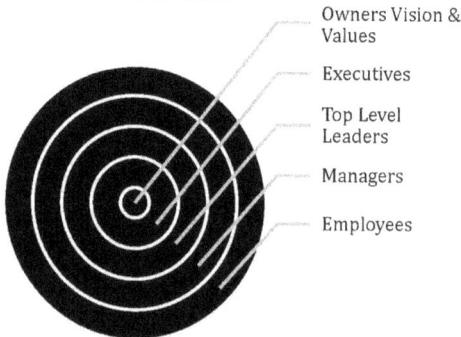

Owners Vision & Values
Executives
Top Level Leaders
Managers
Employees

HOW THE CIRCLE THEORY WORKS

The Circle Theory works on building a solid foundation starting with the core. In this case, it would be the company's vision and values. It is important that the circle start from the core since the foundation is built on what the owners believe and where they see the company's future is headed. As simple as this may sound, many companies take it for granted that those beliefs alone are sufficient to create a sustainable infrastructure. The problem is that once that core is established, as the company's vision and values, a mission statement or something to that effect is hung on the wall and only referred to again when it's convenient. Instead, the vision and values that make up the core of the company need to be seen as its lifeblood, flowing through everything the company does to reflect its core essence.

Surrounded by the company's visions and values are the top level executives. These people should embody the core message and be the best example of what the company is trying to accomplish. Through them, the core message should spread throughout the organization, and ultimately, to the end user or consumer.

Many times, companies will hire someone who has a great ability or talent and put that person in a top level executive position. The talented individual's experience and business acumen may bring temporary results, but if the person is not aligned with the company's values and vision, the message being sent throughout the organization becomes confusing and unclear.

AN APPLE A DAY

In 1985, Steve Jobs, co-founder and chief executive of Apple, lost a struggle with then CEO John Scully and left Apple. During Jobs' absence from 1985 to 1997, Apple seemed to flounder in the computer market with no clear direction. During these years, Apple lost the original vision of its founders and was not able to bring the cohesiveness together to continue promoting a clear brand for the company.

Michael Spindler and Gil Amelio succeeded Scully respectively until Apple, in late 1996, purchased NeXT, owned by Steve Jobs, which resulted in Jobs returning to Apple as interim CEO in 1997. After Jobs' return, Apple began to see a return to profitability as early as 1998.

In 2010, Apple, under Steve Jobs, became strong; some say it arguably surpassed Microsoft in market value for the first time in its history. According to the *New York Times* May 26, 2010 edition, Wall Street valued Apple at $222.12 billion and Microsoft at $219.18 billion.

You may be thinking, "Who really cares when you get into the billions in market value?" What is important is the process that got the company there. If you look at the core of Apple in its early stages, during Steve Jobs' absence, compared to after his return, it signifies the importance of the Circle Theory and its application to business. How well Apple performed was directly related to how well its vision was carried from the leader to the consumer. In other words, t**he rings of the circle continue** as represented in the above model and extend further to include customers, their friends, and others.

WHY IS THE CIRCLE THEORY IMPORTANT?

Why is the Circle Theory more valuable than traditional top to bottom or bottom to top models? This circular model helps to build a company that is centered around its vision and values. The model emphasizes continuity of the company message at each level before moving to the next ring. At some point, if the model is built correctly, hundreds, thousands, or maybe even millions of people will come to believe in the "brand" you have created, based on the company's vision and values. The beauty of this situation is if someone tries to challenge or tries to create negative feedback about a product or service, all those believers will defend the company. They also act as salespeople for the organization.

Think of Apple today versus ten years ago. How many followers does the company now have? When you talk to Apple devotees, how passionate are they about the product and future products, and how well do they know the differences in the product line? The followers I have spoken to will defend Apple's products as if they owned stock in the company (maybe they do); they could easily work for Apple as sales representatives.

In markets or economies where a boom occurs, such as in the dot-com era or in the housing market, a company can build a financially successful business in a very short time. However, when that happens, they create a thin shell around the business. As times change and become more challenging, the ability to sustain the business through employee motivation and customer loyalty becomes very difficult. That is when you usually see a lot of blaming and less self-responsibility.

A false shell is created with each ring of the circle, and although it appears to be solid, it is in reality, fragile. Over time, the shells eventually will crack and crumble and the business will come crashing down.

I witnessed this firsthand in a business where I was a partner. The business did extremely well in the beginning, but the partners did not have the same vision, values, and personal integrity. Confusion at the core created confusion throughout the business and to the customers. It was sad to see this situation happening. You could see that employees wanted to do well and make a difference, but in a partnership, when the core of the circle is not unified, it will eventually crumble. Because the other partners and I could not agree on the company's vision, I left the business and moved on.

THERE IS A FUTURE

We'd like to know what will happen in our future. That's why we plan for retirement, save money for vacations, and plan for the kids' college tuitions. In business, if employees don't know what's happening, they end up guessing and the business ends up losing. The Circle Theory and model allow everyone to know where the company's future is headed, and in a sense, it includes each employee in the process as the company moves forward. The individual employee's job is then no longer just a day-to-day experience; it becomes a career.

Not everyone will buy into the model and believe in the business' values and vision, regardless of what the owners do. Employees may stray off the path once in awhile. A leader's job is to encourage the employees to come back and follow the way of the business. If, at some point, the employees still continue on their own paths, it will be time to part ways. It's not good or bad; it just is.

WHAT ABOUT ME?

At this point, you may be thinking, "But I don't own a business; I work for somebody, so how does the Circle Theory and model apply to me?" Great question!

Everybody is unique, and each person's reality revolves around him- or herself at the core. You are no different. The model can be used for your personal, professional, or spiritual life, or a combination of your life as a whole. In the center of your circle would be you and your Source of Divine Presence. The next few rings would be whatever is most important in your life. They may include a spouse or partner, and then your children, if you have any. The other rings would represent everything you do, who you are, and what is important to you.

Bringing who you are to what you do is how you live your best, best life. In other words, living your passion and carrying that life-invigorating energy to all areas of your life allows you to be the best you can be. Building a solid foundation in your life becomes your support system in times of need. The truer you are to your own values, passion, and purpose, the higher the quality of the rings and people you attract to your circle.

If you have been through a divorce, or you know a couple who have been together for a long time but all of a sudden get divorced, you have seen how divorce can affect people's lives. The couple may have been together for the sake of the kids, sacrificed doing what they loved until the kids grew up, or put the kids before their own relationship, but at some point, they came to realize that they had built a fragile shell that was not representative of the life they wanted to live.

Changes at times may be very subtle so that a person may not even be aware of the changes. That is when others may be noticing the person changing and even point it out to him or her, but the person fails or refuses to acknowledge it's true until something drastic happens. Then the person "wakes up" one day and realizes life has passed him by. Some try to mask this situation or go into denial by using alcohol, drugs, or adrenaline-stimulating activities of high risk, or by completely ignoring the truth.

FATHER KNOWS BEST

Have you ever been told when living under someone else's roof that you need to live by that person's rules? I have. My parents had their own circles they developed through their upbringing, circumstances, and experiences. In their beliefs, not getting a college eduction did not fit into the Circle Theory they developed.

Little did my father know I was lost. I had no clue what I wanted to do or study so I opted to work. As I brought my teenage years to a close, when I didn't work, I partied, had fun, and enjoyed a reckless life. Obviously, out of concern for my well-being and direction in life, my father pointed out that my actions did not fit into how he had created his life. Although I did not know it at the time, it was not wrong that he believed that; it was simply who he was. His rules just didn't resonate with me. I masked my indifference with alcohol and partying, not knowing how to express what was important to me.

IGNITE YOUR BRILLIANCE - BUILD YOUR BEST LIFE MODEL!

Surround yourself with what matters most to you in your life, the people you love and people who support you in your efforts and dreams, even through the ups and downs. Build a network of people who believe not only in what you stand for, but in you.

THE CORE

In the center of your circle, place yourself and your Source of Divine Presence. Ask yourself these questions:

What do I believe about my Source of Divine Presence?

_____

_____

_____

_____

_____

_____

When I die, what would I like the world to know about me?

_____

_____

_____

_____

_____

_____

My Values:

a. _____   b. _____

c. _____   d. _____

e. _____   f. _____

g. _____   h. _____

i. _____   j. _____

What do I believe to be true?

_____

_____

_____

_____

_____

What do I stand for?

_____

_____

_____

_____

What positive impact do I want to make in the world?

_____

_____

_____

_____

_____

What am I grateful for?

_____

_____

_____

_____

_____

_____

The First Ring

This ring begins the core of your circle. You can create the life you want starting today. Who are the top ten people who believe in and support you?

1. _____   2. _____

3. _____   4. _____

5. _____   6. _____

7. _____   8. _____

9. _____   10. _____

This first ring can also be just one person, a cause, or a non-profit organization or charity as well.

THE SUCCESSIVE RINGS

Continue to add rings with relationships that matter and support your endeavors and beliefs. Respect others whose beliefs do not resonate with you and avoid anyone who is vexatious to your spirit. Do not include those who refuse to change and continue to bring you down, rain on your parade, or do not value the human spirit. Respect wisdom and integrity and reflect humility. Be grateful wherever you are in your journey. Forgive those who have tripped you in your path and thank them for whatever gift they left you.

You are magnificent, and you are meant to share your gifts with the world regardless of how young or old you are. You are here to share your brilliance with the world and to let your light shine. **This is your time to take action and Ignite Your Brilliance!**

CHAPTER ELEVEN

INSPIRED LEADERSHIP

A leader is a dealer in hope.
~Napoleon Bonaparte

How do you define leadership? When you hear the word "leadership," what comes to your mind? Leadership is often associated with business and the corporate world, but in reality, everyone is a leader. Think about your life after you became an adult. You are responsible for your life, the direction you're headed, and for your happiness.

Your association with leadership may have come from:

- Your own personal experiences
- Your parents
- Observations and dealings with a boss, coworkers, or managers who represented authority
- The media's headlines about people in power and the events they shape
- Teachers and schools
- Books, tapes, CDs, or DVDs on leadership

Many great books on leadership are in the marketplace today. Everyone has his or her slant on what leadership means and how best to apply or utilize the skills and tenets that define and empower individuals.

An old image of leadership, the slam your fist on the table and do as I say template, was an intimidation tactic that more or less created ill will toward those in charge. Thirty years ago, although I did not really know what true leadership was, I knew I didn't like the way employees were being treated by their bosses. The style of leadership being displayed was neither inspiring nor effective.

Being exposed to this kind of leadership tattooed an impression on me that was hidden between my skin and my soul. Its effects were so ingrained in my consciousness. Professionally, I worked hard to avoid the "old style" of leadership and challenged its presenters when I came across them. I worked hard at integrating leadership with teams.

WHAT IS INSPIRED LEADERSHIP?

Inspired leadership is about creating an environment that is conducive to individual growth where the collective potential of individuals is brought together to work toward a common good or goal. This leadership style is rooted in core values that honor individuals as unique contributors. It also represents the highest integrity and recognizes the human element that moves beyond structure as important to true success.

THE TRIAD OF INSPIRED LEADERSHIP (TIL)

VISION

LEADER

STRUCTURE/SYSTEMS   THE HUMAN ELEMENT

Vision: A vision is the creation of a visual image that represents the realization and manifestation of your thoughts. A vision can be compared to a paint-by-number work of art. We visualize the final picture and direct which color or attribute goes where. As a leader, you determine how you fill in the numbers or colors through your systems and structure.

Structure/Systems: Structure and systems define the when, where, who, and how of this marvelous picture (vision) that you have created.

The Human Element: Human beings are the variables that determine the degree of success in manifesting your vision.

HOW THE TRIAD OF LEADERSHIP APPLIES TO YOU

	PERSONALLY	**PROFESSIONALLY**
Vision:	Your Ultimate Dreams	Company Future
	Your Best Life	Your Aspirations
	Freedom	Happiness
	Living Authentically	Operating with Integrity

Structure/ Systems:	The roadmap to achieving your dreams	The plan and infrastructure that support your vision
The Human Element:	How and who can best support you during this journey	Identifies the key elements that nurture and utilize the team's strength

MR. GALLO AND CHEMISTRY CLASS

Mr. Gallo, my high school chemistry teacher, was an inspiration to me. Although I had many good teachers, he stood out. He was an excellent teacher, not because he was easy, but because he held a high standard for his students that he knew we were capable of attaining. He was funny, entertaining, and he called himself, "The Fox" because he told us we would never be able to outsmart him.

Mr. Gallo would always remind us that we were the "cream of the crop," and because we were the best, he expected the best from us. He inspired us by his method of leadership. He mixed interesting experiments into his instruction, and he always acknowledged what we did right. I looked forward to his classes. It's no surprise that Mr. Gallo went on to receive an award for placing the most students in college for degrees in chemistry.

Mr. Gallo was successfully able to manage each section of the Triad of Leadership. He understood each student's need to be a unique individual, and he incorporated that into his program's vision and structure. He was able to bring together the collective potential of all his students so they could learn from each other as well from him.

The 5-P Matrix

The elements of the 5-P Matrix support and encourage the inspired leader to excel at a level that moves beyond the ego. It creates a solid foundation that is sustainable through any economy or market changes, and at the end of the day, it brings fulfillment through what is created.

1. Purpose with Passion

2. People

3. Plan

4. Persistence

5. Profit

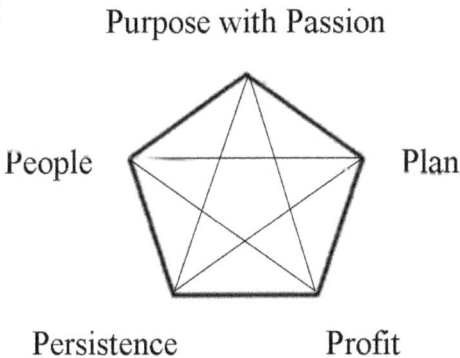

Purpose with Passion

People

Plan

Persistence   Profit

1. Passion and Purpose

It's a very simple concept yet profound reality that if you do not like the activities you perform in your profession, the chances of your being happy in life are slim to none. As we discussed in a previous chapter, unhappiness is not something you can hide.

Many determinants support our choices: ego, money, status in the community, family legacy, laziness, complacency, and passion, just to name a few. If you are passionate about what you do, chances are you will be more persistent through the tough times, economic fluctuations, and potential roadblocks that are a part of life and business. Passion lends itself to commitment.

Most of us strive to find purpose and meaning in our lives that ultimately bring happiness and fulfillment. Having a purpose to which we are infinitely connected anchors our Spirit to a place that becomes unshakeable. Even through life's trials and tribulations, purpose helps to keep us focused on what's important in our lives, to keep our heads up and looking toward a future that will reflect the reality we choose to create. Our purpose is the focus that brings forth our greatest good and what we want to achieve in this lifetime.

Inspired leadership is about taking any situation and making the best of it. If you are in a position that does not reflect your ultimate happiness, challenge yourself to understand why and to create what works.

You can start by being mindful. Mindfulness teaches us that it is possible to take a moment to observe the reactions of our body, mind, heart, and spirit at any moment in our lives. Understanding this reality in connection to what you do allows you to approach where you are from a different perspective.

Being a great steward of the gifts you are given will prove to those around you and to your Source of Divine Presence that you are capable of handling and accepting more.

2. People

Human beings are the cornerstone of life. Because diversity does not allow any two people to be exactly alike, it lends itself to creating an opportunity to provide the company with a distinct value. Too often, companies tend to drift toward blurring the uniqueness of individuals into a living template under the guise of making things easier to manage and control. Molding people into conformity can, to some degree, work as nicely as taking tea and putting it into bags and then boxing it. It provides a sense of consistent results, but it may also make all the tea look the same. When people are molded into conformity, we lose sense of their true meaning and individual talents just as we may neglect to realize that the tea in each individual tea bag has its own unique and delicious flavor.

It is easy to take someone who is already good at what he does and help him grow, but it takes a true leader to bring out the gifts and talents from someone who may not recognize his own gifts.

3. Plan

A plan is a road map outlining the path to your vision and success. The road map is important so you can keep track of your intended destination. That's not to say that the path may change over time, but it helps to have a guide on how to get there, and when obstacles appear, it brings the confidence needed to overcome it through commitment of vision.

Although it may depend on the nature of your project or vision, simple is always better. The simpler the plan, the easier it will be to communicate it to others. The easier the communication, the more likely others will understand your intent and you will be supported. The same holds true for both personal and professional endeavors.

4. Persistence

So many times, great ideas, plans, dreams, and visions disappear just before people achieve success. Too often, difficulties cause people to give up just before they would have succeeded. Persistence in following through and having the resilience to overcome obstacles, doubts, and fears can take you through those barriers.

If you believe in what you are doing, how deep are you willing to go within yourself to find what it takes to move you to the next plateau? How connected are you to your Source of Divine Presence, and how much faith and trust do you have in that Source to support you through the rough times so it will make a difference in the outcome?

It's amazing how persistent most children are in trying to find an answer to a question or to satisfy their curiosity. They can be relentless in their persistence and will not stop until they reach their goals or are stopped by well-intentioned parents.

Are you willing to let the same tenacity you had as a child infuse your life and become your accountability partner?

5. Profit

Does the word "profit" sound so corporate that it becomes a turn off? If it does, then change the word to whatever serves you, such as: outcome, end result, or success. Whatever word you choose, whether it is for your business or your life, profit needs to exist in order to live a balanced life.

Some people treat the word "profit" as if it were a dirty word. You make a profit if you have the ability to spend less money than you make. It's that simple. The only other option to create a profit is to generate more money (and I don't mean getting your laser printer and printing more.) I mean finding other sources of income—multiple streams.

Having money is not a "cure all," but it is a start. It can even be viewed as a spiritual experience and process. Everything in this world is a form of energy. Money is no different. It is our perception and relationship to money that creates our reality.

THE LOVE OF LEADING

The inspired leader is able to weave the tapestry of the above matrix into a holistic forward movement. The orchestrated movement of an organization toward a greater vision focuses on solutions and creates a distinctive value unique to that particular business.

It is of the utmost importance that all five elements of the 5-P Matrix are included as key areas in the inspired leader's program. Emphasis of a well-integrated matrix leads to a long-term sustainable business. The leader understands the dynamics that each sector brings to the "whole" of the business, but he recognizes that no one sector can sustain the business alone.

It starts at the core. The person at the organization's core is the inspired leader. The leader is someone who has the passion and who identifies the purpose that can be articulated and communicated through the organization to the end user. The leader understands the need to release the ego and bring on people who are much more skilled than he or she is, with the understanding that the leader still makes the final decision on the path to success.

5-P AND YOU

Take the time to look at how the 5-P Matrix can apply to your personal life. Whether you are a parent, employee, entrepreneur, or executive, the 5-P Matrix can be applied to your life. Write down how it applies in each area.

Passion & Purpose

_____

_____

_____

_____

_____

_____

_____

People

_____

_____

_____

_____

_____

_____

_____

Plan

_____

_____

_____

_____

_____

_____

_____

Persistence

_____
_____
_____
_____
_____
_____
_____

Profit

_____
_____
_____
_____
_____
_____

Summary

The best leadership style is one that resonates with who you are and what you believe in. Ask yourself, "Are the lives of the people I lead enhanced or stifled?" Monitor your progress by looking at how balanced the lives are of the people you lead. Do you see more smiles than frowns? Are your employees inspired to want to do more and succeed? Are creative ideas flowing within your team?

Check in with the 5-P Matrix and adjust accordingly. Continue to be your best and express your Brilliance through Balance so others recognize it and allow themselves to do the same.

CHAPTER TWELVE

CHANGE – THE EGO'S NEMESIS

Change is inevitable—except from a vending machine.
~ Robert C. Gallagher

The carving of our existence into the landscape of time is a reflection of the role we choose to play in our story. Whoa, now there's a sentence! We are the creators of this amazing life, and we have the opportunity to bring the best out of every situation so we live a happy, natural, and vibrant life.

Change is inevitable and as natural as the unfolding of life. We observe change every day. The grass grows, the trees change, leaves fall, and different birds and animals visit your home. We pass by different people every time we go somewhere.

The sun rises and sets. Every twenty-four hours, we get to begin again with a new day that turns into a new week, a new month, and a new year. Each day brings a new perspective, more opportunities, and a chance for greater appreciation of life!
~ Jeffery Bow

Are you willing to let go of the past and the future to celebrate what life has to offer you today?

Change often stirs up emotions and we begin to question our current state of life. Do you find yourself saying at times, "I had more money back then," "I wish I could have," "I don't have the skills they have," or "I should be _____ in my life"? Letting go of the past and the future of what you "should" be, do, or should have done allows you to focus completely on the present and what's important to you now, the only time there really is.

Seasons change. If you are currently out of work, not where you want to be in life, or you have a larger vision for yourself, know that where you are is only temporary. You have everything within you right now to live your best life. Do not define who you are by your current circumstances, good or bad, because there's always movement in life.

WHY HAS THE PROCESS OF "CHANGE" BECOME SUCH A HUGE FACTOR IN OUR LIVES?

Our minds are wired for consistency. Our brain challenges change or inconsistencies until we are exposed to them so many times that we come to see them as consistent. Once we view them as consistent, we come to believe they are true.

Think about what keeps you going back to the same restaurant for more. It is the consistency of the food, service, and atmosphere that delivers a similar message to your brain each time you have an experience there. Franchises are successful because they have a system that delivers consistent results each and every time. Not only do franchises produce those results at that one location, but they can produce the same results at any of their locations.

How about when you were dating? When you liked someone, you noticed the positive things in that person each and every time you looked at him or her or talked to the person on the phone. You saw 150 percent good in the object of your affection. To make sure the attraction was mutual, you looked for signs that the other person liked you too. Consistency of those positive traits reinforced your liking for one another.

In business, new programs, new people, and new ideas can either bring inspiration or doubt. Our instinctive nature is to doubt because it disrupts the flow of consistency in our minds and the comfort level of our ego. Just when you think you have it down, something new comes along. "Not again" you may be thinking.

Identify the Top Five Changes you recognize you are going through at the moment:

1._____

2._____

3._____

4._____

5._____

The foundation of your values is tested through change.
Change brings awareness to what is important and allows you
to reexamine your path to fulfillment.
~ Jeff Bow

CHANGE BRINGS OPPORTUNITY!

Change is a gift we can accept or deny. With the gift comes a greater potential to elevate our awareness of what is important in our lives. With change, we expand our minds through learning, exploration of new possibilities, and innovation, and we increase our connection to our Source of Divine Presence.

At the time that change occurs, our ego may deny us from accessing the value that the change may bring. We may even find ourselves resisting or even denying that the change is needed. After our initial ego-trum (ego tantrum), a time comes when you realize an opportunity exists for you to grow from this experience on some level. You have the power necessary to find the value in the situation and translate that value to elevate your level of consciousness. Elevating your level of consciousness brings you closer to happiness, and ultimately, to fulfillment.

An example that pulls at the heart strings is the death of a loved one. Our humanity, closeness, and love for that person make us want him or her to be around forever. However, we know in our logical mind that at some point everyone will transition into another realm (You may call it Heaven, another world, another lifetime, etc.). Although you cannot reverse the situation, you may look at your own life in retrospect and think of things that make you appreciate life even more. We may want to say, "I love you" more often to our family members and friends and not wait until it's too late. We may look at our own health and decide that we want to take action and be proactive in living a healthy lifestyle. We may find it to be a wakeup call for celebrating what we have and to enjoying life now instead of focusing on what we don't have. We may rediscover the value of true friends.

Whatever the situation, try your best to find the secret that is communicated through change, for it is truly a gift waiting for you.

What value have you found in your Top Five Changes (listed earlier)?

1._____

2._____

3._____

4._____ _____

5._____

BIRD BRAIN

Have you ever gone up to a parrot and repeatedly said, "Hello"? After no response, you may have given up because the parrot didn't feel like talking or it couldn't. I have done this, but at other times, parrots are willing to repeat what people say often and at unexpected times, or they'll say things their owners don't want them to repeat in front of guests. According to a January 17, 2006 article on CNN.com, a man found out that his girlfriend was having an affair after his parrot, named Ziggy, kept on repeating her lover's name. Being called a birdbrain is not so bad after all!

RÉPÉTEZ S'IL VOUS PLAÎT

Parrots learn through repetition. People learn through repetition as well. Recognition becomes ingrained in us through the consistency of repetition. Although statistics vary, some say that it takes five to seven exposures before people will notice or buy into something. Think about situations you see on an everyday basis, either in your personal or work life, or on commercials or in print advertising. It's all about repetition, repetition, repetition! Repetition brings about "top of the mind" awareness. Do you remember those loud commercials that were repeated over and over during the same show you watched on TV? They became subconsciously imbedded in your mind. When you hear the beginning of a familiar song that you used to listen to when you were younger, you recognize the song right away. It automatically brings you back to the time and place when you used to hear that song. Along with the song come back memories, emotions, and feelings associated with that experience.

CHANGE AS A GPS

For those of us who have used a GPS and have taken a wrong turn, we have heard the GPS navigating voice say, "Recalculating." It will keep repeating itself until you get on the right street and back on track.

Change can do the same thing for us. With each circumstance that change brings, it allows us to reevaluate the current path we are on, whether it's with our finances, work, relationships, extreme self-care, self-development or spirituality.

Changes at your work may occur often with the fluctuating economy, the need to stay competitive, to continue to be innovators, or to be more profitable. We may or may not agree with the changes at first, but as time goes on, if we continually disagree with the changes, perhaps that's our own internal GPS signaling us to reexamine our path and dreams. We may have hidden desires and dreams of owning our own cafe, restaurant, yoga studio, or other business. Perhaps we were sidetracked by well meaning people who said we would never make money at our dream; it was too risky, so we should stick to our day jobs. Eventually, so we can live lives of fulfillment, these messages to follow our dreams keep coming back until we take the time to explore them.

Exploring our dreams doesn't mean that we make foolish decisions, quit our job, or take unnecessary risks. It means that we first determine whether it's what we really want or whether it's something that is ego-driven. Many people envy actors for what notoriety, money, and fame can bring. When we look at the other side of that image, actors lose their privacy, always need security guards, and have a tremendous amount of pressure to be young and vibrant forever. We can explore our dreams further to determine what resonates with our values and spiritual self so we don't end up on the wrong path where what we thought we wanted leads to unhappiness. A good dream will give us choices, opportunities, and a strong possibility for happiness.

SUMMARY

Part of taking action is change. Change allows you to create a different path, correct the one you are on, or modify it so it is in alignment with your current intentions.

It is not always easy or comforting to go through change. Many times others are affected along the way, but that creates an opportunity for them to change as well. Change can stir up hidden emotions that surface in the form of fear. As you recognize and honor those emotions and break through fear, you realize a sense of freedom.

Your ability to navigate change is phenomenal. Staying true to the essence of who you are through the process provides stability during the shaky times. When you release the expectation and control of the outcome, the transformative energy that results can be beautiful and rewarding.

The previous sections covered the creation of your vision and dreams and your connection with your body, mind, and spirit. By embracing change, you move closer to your ultimate life of joy, happiness, and fulfillment. Embrace change by following your heart.

SECTION FOUR

ACCEPTANCE

*Out beyond ideas of wrong doing and right doing, there
is a field. I will meet you there.*
~ Jalal ad-Din Rumi

★ CHAPTER THIRTEEN ★

FUN

I never did a day's work in my life. It was all fun.
~ Thomas A. Edison

When was the last time you had real fun, spontaneous fun?

Do you remember when you were a child and you looked forward to recess? As you grew older you looked forward to summer vacations. As a working adult, you love Fridays because you know the weekend is near. Everyone seems to be a bit nicer, happier, and more tolerant knowing the weekend is about to start. Periodic vacations also are times to which we look forward.

Why is it that as we grow older, our dedicated time to have fun becomes less and less? The seriousness of work and life begin to dissolve our fun time so we can make room for the more "adult responsibilities." It seems like we get through the days, weeks, and months just so we can enjoy some time off to relax and have some fun.

When I was sixteen years old, I worked at my uncle's service station. One slow evening when no customers were around, we decided to have shopping cart races around the pumps. We had a blast! But the next day, we were called into the office by my uncle. He reprimanded us for playing and goofing off. Someone had squealed on us! Was my uncle wrong in his reaction? Absolutely not! He had invested a lot of money buying the service station, and he had placed his trust in me to represent the company as he had envisioned it. Although what we did was foolish, we still knew how to have fun and we weren't afraid to express it.

When I used to watch funny television shows like *I Love Lucy* or films with the Three Stooges, or Jerry Lewis and Dean Martin, my father warned me not to watch the shows too much or I would become just like the people on them. And he was right! I love to have fun!

What were some of the fun things you did as a child?

_____

_____

_____

_____

_____

_____

_____

_____

So what is wrong with this picture? The business environment when I was growing up was about being serious and formal. High-end restaurant servers wore tuxedos and embraced the attitude of being "snooty" as the way to treat customers. It was not right or wrong, good or bad; it was just in vogue at the time. This description of that time is not to downplay those who struggled to survive, build a business, or create a better life for their families. It is the recognition of how our environment infiltrates our consciousness and ultimately our happiness. It has the potential to remove our innate sense of "fun" that we knew as a child.

THE SHIFT

Fast forwarding to today, too many people work their entire lives to save and plan for the big trip of their dreams once they retire, only to find out that they are out of time, and they were never able to realize their dreams. They have led unhappy lives, merely existing rather than living their lives to the fullest. Because of their unhappiness, their view of the world became a negative cloud that followed them wherever they went.

People rarely succeed unless they have fun in what they are doing.
~ Dale Carnegie

Most people and businesses forget to have fun. However, it has been my experience that a direct correlation exists between fun and bottom line profits in business. Have you ever noticed that crowds gather around happy, fun people? I am reminded of the California Milk commercial theme, "Happy cows produce better milk."

Fun should be an inclusive, not exclusive, part of our lives. Even work should be fun. We should be able to have appropriate fun at work and enjoy what we do. Google has consistently ranked in the Top Five of Fortune-CNN Money's 100 Best Places to Work because it has created the atmosphere of a college campus where the employees not only work hard, but they relax and have fun. The company provides opportunities to learn, grow, travel, and have wild, zany fun during the workday, according to a Great Places to Work Institute article titled, "Why is Google so Great?"[1] It's not surprising that the question arises whether Google is listed as a best place to work because of its stock prices or whether its stock prices are high as a result of what it has created in its work environment.

An article by Patricia Bathurst from June 1, 2008 in *Arizona Business and Money*, titled "Having Fun at Work Increases Loyalty and Productivity"[2] cited a study by Ipsos that surveyed 1,000 employees. The study found that in companies where the managers' humor was rated "above average," the employees were likely to stay longer. The study also concluded that this trend of fun in business was a push from workers who want a better work-life balance. Many companies also found that fun increased their bottom line.

REV UP THE FUN IN YOUR LIFE!

First and foremost, balance your life! It's difficult to have fun if something is weighing on your mind. Start the process of looking at your life balance, and take small steps to integrate balance into your life so you get the process and energy moving. Moving energy creates momentum, flow, and confidence to try other things. Review Chapter 8: Brilliance Through Balance.

Focus on what's working! Look at the things that *are* working in your life. It would be easy to gravitate toward the negative, but that does not support forward movement in your life.

1 Lashinsky, Adam. "Google is No. 1: Search and enjoy." January 10, 2007. http://money.cnn.com/2007/01/05/magazines/fortune/Search_and_enjoy.fortune/. Accessed April 14, 2011.
2 http://www.azcentral.com/business/articles/2008/06/01/20080601biz-funat-work0601-ON.html. Accessed April 14, 2011.

Negativity weighs us down and keeps us digging a deeper hole, much like a car stuck in the mud. The tires spin, but the car stays in the same place. Review Chapter 3: What We Focus on Expands.

Change it up! Do something different. Instead of the "same old, same old" routine, try something new. Trying new things doesn't need to cost a lot of money. Visit places where you normally would not go unless you had guests in town and you were showing them around. Be a tourist in your own backyard. It's amazing what you will discover and how fun it can be. Learn another language and plan a trip. Try a new restaurant or new recipe. Spend a day outdoors. Plan a dream vacation. Build something. Express yourself through art—paint, write, or draw. The possibilities are endless.

What can you add to the list of possibilities?

1. _____	2. _____	3. _____
4. _____	5. _____	6. _____
7. _____	8. _____	9. _____
10. _____	11. _____	12. _____
13. _____	14. _____	15. _____

Laugh, laugh, laugh. Although it's debatable, some say that children laugh 300-400 times a day versus adults only laughing fifteen times per day. The short- and long-term benefits of laughter are well-documented. According to the Mayo Clinic[3], some of the positive benefits of laughter include helping to

3 http://www.mayoclinic.com/health/stress-relief/SR00034.
Accessed April 17, 2011.

stimulate the organs, activating and relieving stress response, soothing tension, improving the immune system, relieving pain, and increasing personal satisfaction. Laughter is nature's way of creating balance in our bodies. It relieves system overload.

Laughter is contagious! Have you ever been around someone who couldn't stop laughing? The person laughed so hard that he or she began to cry. I know I have done that myself, and soon afterwards, others started laughing. Think about how you feel after a good laugh. Laughter is a wonderful act of our innate nature. Laughter leads to joy and happiness.

Facial expressions bring on certain emotions. Make a sad face and see how you feel. Then, smile and see how your body language influences your emotions.

SUMMARY

Life is too short not to have fun along the way. Having fun in every part of your life means that what you are doing resonates with who you are. At that moment, there is a flow. It moves you, takes you away from your mind, and opens your heart.

If you are not having fun in your life, think about what is missing. I invite you to take the time to become truly aware of what is working in your life and what is not. Accept where you are now; then move forward to create the life you have always wanted and dreamed of living. It is never too late. You are resourceful, creative, and empowered. Give yourself the permission to enjoy life. Now is your time.

★ CHAPTER FOURTEEN ★

COLLABORATION

The secret is to gang up on the problem, rather than each other.
~ Thomas Stallkamp

Collaboration is a way of bringing people together to express and share, motivate and inspire, change or create. You have taken action and are waiting for the fruits of your labor to come forward, and now you are ready to take action with others for even greater results without fear or worry because you have reached the Acceptance stage where people come to the realization that everything happens in its right time and place. Acceptance is the understanding on all levels that where you are in this exact time and place is where you are supposed to be in your life.

YEAH, BUT!

The word "Gremlins," used as a coaching term, means your self-doubting thoughts, negative thinking, and other obstacles that prevent you from breaking through fear. Some of these Gremlins may be comparing yourself to others who are more or sometimes less successful than yourself. Staying in a state of

"I should have done this" or saying to yourself, "If I had done this, I would be there by now" will not move you forward. These Gremlins weigh you down and are a waste of energy that could otherwise be used to move you forward in persistence and breaking through the fear that binds you from your full expression.

Collaboration is a way to support you to know that you are not alone in this world of life. There are many others who have gone through or are going through what you are experiencing. Through collaboration, you still may find inspiration, ideas, and other valuable tips to help you continue your journey.

Examples of how well collaboration works in organizations can be seen in Rotary and Lions Clubs, Building Industry Associations, Better Business Bureaus, the Red Cross, AAA–Automobile Associations, AAA—Alcohol Treatment Programs, HOA—Homeowners Associations, HOG—Harley Owners Group, car clubs, restaurant associations, alumni associations, cooking groups, gardening clubs, non-profit organizations, entrepreneurial groups, and thousands of others right in your own neighborhood.

These businesses base their structures on collaborative efforts such as network marketing and franchised businesses. These business structures provide a proven method of success that offers structure, support, and a connection to others we can turn to who can relate to similar experiences. Businesses with multiple branches and geographical diversity use collaboration as a means to learn, grow, and communicate effectively in a similar fashion to franchises.

A recent search on Amazon.com using the word "collaboration" came up with 9,787 books with collaboration in their content. Google produced 112,000,000 results with the word collaboration. These results reflect how many resources are out there to support you in the collaborative process you are going through at this very moment.

FEAR OF THE UNKNOWN

Fear of the unknown is one of the biggest factors that prevents us from breaking through and igniting our brilliance. Generally, if we do not know what to do or where we are headed, we guess, and in doing so, we have fear and uncertainty that cause us to gravitate toward negativity and scarcity. The relinquishing of control to accept a state of not knowing can be very difficult for some people.

What are your top five situations or problems at this moment that you do not have answers or solutions for so they are bringing you fear? Write them in the form of a question, such as "How do I pay my bills while working on my dream?"

1. _____

2. _____

3. _____

4. _____

5. _____

TURN YOUR PROBLEMS INTO SOLUTIONS!

Now, for each item above, reframe the question into a solution. For example, "How do I pay my bills while working on my dream?" can be turned into, "I will look for others who are successful who have started off in the same way and follow their examples or advice."

1. _____

2. _____

3. _____

4. _____

5. _____

Name three organizations, resources, or people for each solution that you can collaborate with to build confidence so you can be persistent in pursuing your dreams. Identifying these people or groups will expand your resource base and help you to focus on and look at where you want to be rather than where you are. You can use the same organizations more than once if they can be solutions to multiple questions.

Example Question: How do I pay my bills while working on my dream?

Example Solution: I will look for others who are successful who have started off in the same way and follow their example or advice.

Example Resources:

a. Local Rotary

b. Entrepreneur and Success Magazine subscriptions

c. Local industry organization for networking.

Identify your resources:

1 – a. _____ b. _____ c. _____

2 – a. _____ b. _____ c. _____

3 – a. _____ b. _____ c. _____

4 – a. _____ b. _____ c. _____

5 – a. _____ b. _____ c. _____

See whether you have identified an organization or resource multiple times. That would be a great place to start. Determine the amount of time you can devote to working on the area of collaboration. Addressing all the solutions at once may be overwhelming. Start off with the easiest and what is most beneficial to you.

Sometimes on the way to our dreams, we get lost
and find an even better dream.
~ Unknown

Collaboration may bring amazing surprises as long as you are open to the process. You may discover and unfold a creative, better, and more joyful way of accomplishing your dreams. You can never go wrong because there is no wrong way to fulfill a dream. Consciously having fun on your journey will bring vibrancy to your life.

THE UNIQUENESS OF SNOW

It is miraculous how no two snowflakes are alike. Each is utterly unique, yet when together, they blanket the ground and form a spectacular landscape. When joined with other snowflakes, the newly formed collaboration provides a surface for us to enjoy through skiing, snowboarding, snowmobiling, ice fishing, making snow angels and snowman, and other various winter activities.

Similarly, no two humans are alike. When people are brought together, the power of their collaboration compounds and creates a momentum that exudes unity.

THE EGO RETURNS

The one thing that may prevent someone from participating in collaboration is ego. Ego wants us to stand out and be the hero, be recognized, and be propelled into superstar status. One of the myths or fears we have surrounding collaboration, caused by our ego, is that we will lose our identity and uniqueness.

> *Being in a band is always a compromise.*
> *Provided that the balance is good,*
> *what you lose in compromise, you gain by collaboration.*
> ~ Mike Rutherford

Even when we collaborate or we use other people's ideas or lessons, we can never lose what resides in our heart. We may adapt those parts that resonate with us from what others teach us, but even then, we make it our own. We can never lose what resides in our heart. Others can try to copy or replicate our ideas, but our uniqueness is what makes the difference and cannot be copied. Holding ourselves in the light of abundance rather than scarcity, and using the model of "learn, do, and teach," helps to overcome the ego's gravitational pull and allow our Source of Divine Presence to work through us.

FRIENDS, FRIENDS, AND MORE FRIENDS

We can never have enough friends! Let me say this again. You can never have enough friends. Too often when we meet people and consider entering a relationship with them, we have the mindset, "What's in it for me?" But our friendships will be more successful when we give up the need to get something out of a relationship and instead get to know others as a part of connecting with them. When we release the "What's in it for me?" mindset, we discover the beauty of true friendship.

True friendships are created through unconditional love and support. They are timeless and effortless. In these friendships, we may not see or talk to someone for over thirty years, but when we see the person again, we pick up right where we left off.

The relationship between true friends is not contingent on anything and judgment has no place. True friendships evolve from the release of any expectations except for one. This one exception is that everyone be true to who he or she is.

FRIENDS - CONNECTION AND COLLABORATION

We are social by nature, so it is natural to come together as a group. We accumulate a true and ever-growing circle of friends, which in turn helps to create a vortex that attracts like-minded individuals to you without effort. These connections may appear out of the blue or when you least expect them. Connections may lead to the collaboration in different forms such as groups, communities, and even partnerships in business and life.

PERCEPTION

Find what works for you. You may even participate in an organization that you find does not resonate with you. That's okay! Move on and look for one that does. It's like shopping for clothes; you may see something on a rack that looks great, but when you try it on, you find it doesn't work for you. So look until you find what does. Whatever works for you is absolutely perfect.

If you look for people or organizations with similar values to your own, it is more likely you will find a greater long-term sustainable relationship than one with differing values.

At times, some collaborative efforts in the form of partnerships may come to an end. Rather than being right or wrong, it's simply that the partnership is no longer useful. How we perceive that reality becomes our experience of the relationship. If we blame others for the partnership or collaboration ending, we may become judgmental and critical when it comes to forming a new collaborative effort. We then may miss out on many future activities. But if we feel only gratitude for the benefits, joy, and time we have enjoyed in collaborating with the other person(s), we will leave feeling enriched and looking forward to the next collaborative opportunity that comes our way. The collaborative efforts I have been involved with have all helped me in some way to be the person I am today—a value that's hard to replace, and I am grateful for all of them.

SUMMARY

Collaboration is an asset when you are feeling the Gremlins creeping in. It can also be a valuable tool for continued support, ideas, connections, and motivation. One of the main points to remember is that what we put into collaboration is what we will get out of it. If you join an organization, work up to the highest position possible that time allows. The higher your visibility, the greater exposure you will receive, and the more connections you will make. As I said earlier, you can never have too many friends.

CHAPTER FIFTEEN

LET GO MY EGO

One may understand the cosmos, but never the ego;
the self is more distant than any star.
~ G. K. Chesterton

"Some people call it 'ego,'
but I think it's art."

How many times have you heard someone say about someone else, "He is so wrapped up in his ego" or "She sure has a big ego"? You probably heard such comments in reference to someone who was viewed as conceited, or worse, the comments were said intentionally to hurt someone else's self-esteem or self-image.

The ego is really not good or bad. The particular circumstance and the judgment we place on someone's behavior are what create a context for our interpretation of someone's ego. The ego is, however, a false self that seeks to protect itself, and it often gets in the way of our true self. Think of the ego as being at one end of a spectrum with the other end being your true self (Spirit, God, Higher Power, or however you choose to define Your Source of Divine Presence). Many use EGO as an acronym for "Edging God Out." The relationship between ego and spirit would look something like this:

EGO ←—————————————→ SPIRIT
(false self)   (true-self)

The ego and spirit are as opposite as night/day, cold/hot, mild/spicy, wet/dry, small/big, or old/new.

It's easier for our own comfort zone to categorize people so they fit into how we understand the world. Categorizing is our way of always having control and feeling we know what is what. When we do not have that ability, it makes us nervous and uncomfortable. When we use the word "egoistic" or say the person has "a big ego," we really are comparing ourselves to that person to boost our own self-esteem; then it's no different than calling someone fat, skinny, stupid, or unworthy.

THE EGO SIDE OF THE SCALE

"... And this one I awarded myself for my overall greatness!"

The ego is about self, the "I" as a separate entity. From the ego's perspective, the world revolves around "me" and is there to serve me. The ego is self-centered, born to be served, demands respect, and creates divisiveness from your true self. The ego lives on attention. The ego side of a person does not recognize spirit first and foremost in itself or others.

The ego bolsters a false reality of the true nature of who we are—it is about the small self. The small self is also, in many ways, a form of denial. It fails to recognize that everyone shares a common connection and no separation exists among us. The ego is the opposite of acceptance.

Acceptance is an important part of breaking through fear and igniting your brilliance. Igniting your brilliance is about bringing who you are, your true self, to what you do in all areas of your life. Living in the ego state limits your ability to connect to your Source of Divine Presence on the highest possible level.

THE SPIRIT SIDE OF THE SCALE

Connection to our Source of Divine Presence is of the utmost importance. At the highest and most connected stage, we are at one with the universe and everyone in the world. There is no separation. There is a realization that geographic isolation or certain genetic traits like skin color cannot separate the connectedness of mankind. It is the recognition and honoring of Spirit in all living creatures, plants, and animals.

Living with this truth on the Spiritual side of the scale brings peace, acceptance, love, joy, and happiness. We focus on what's working and positive. We learn from what is not working, we alter our course, and we move on. There is no blame on the Spiritual plane; there is understanding and self-responsibility. The higher your consciousness, the closer we are to the egoless side of the scale, Spirituality.

Thich Nhat Hanh is a Buddhist monk, teacher, author, poet, and peace activist. He has become an important influence upon Western Buddhism, and his teachings and practices appeal to people from a variety of religious, spiritual, and political backgrounds, offering practices of mindfulness that are more conducive to Western sensibilities.

When Nhat Hanh's book *Living Buddha, Living Christ* was published in 1995, it created controversy because of how it promoted the crossover and integration of religions. Nhat Hanh's purpose was to find value in and similarities between Buddhism and Christianity. He once said, "People deal too much with the negative, with what is wrong. Why not try and see positive things, to just touch those things and make them bloom? In true dialogue, both sides are willing to change."[1]

Thich Nhat Hanh's philosophy is an invitation to peace, love, and harmony. The ability to focus on finding commonalities rather than exploiting the differences brings us to higher levels of consciousness and dissolves barriers that we hold even in our pursuit of our highest ideals.

A SLIDING SCALE

We have the ability to choose our focus and immediately change our mindset and energy. It is a choice, as intellectually easy as yes or no, but we emotionally attach ourselves to a mindset, opinion, or belief out of fear of losing an identity (ego) we have long associated with ourselves, usually as the result of our upbringing, growth, or what we thought to be true.

We have the ability to access any place on the scale of Ego ↔ Spirituality at any time. Throughout our lives we move back and forth, depending on the situation and need. It is the context and intent of our action that defines the state of our being on that scale.

COMEDY AND THE EGO

Seinfeld was a great television comedy sitcom based on observational humor. Its storylines were based on the trivial events of the self-absorbed characters' everyday lives. The characters

---

1 http://www.katinkahesselink.net/tibet/Thich-Nhat-Hanh-love-q.html. Accessed April 20, 2011.

never learned from their experiences, and they were indifferent to the world around them and sometimes to their friends.

I often found myself laughing while watching Seinfeld because I had been in similar situations, or I had acted in a manner similar to the characters when confronted with such situations. Jerry Seinfeld's genius as co-producer brought a lightness to our daily lives when we watched others living in their ego. While we may have difficulty laughing at ourselves when our ego gets out of control, when we can identify people acting like we would when our ego gets out of control, it allows us to laugh at ourselves as well, and when we do that, we realize how ridiculous our ego can be, a good reminder that it's time to gravitate toward the Spiritual side of the scale.

WHERE ARE YOU ON THE SCALE?

Take an honest look to determine where you are on the scale.

Ego   **Spirituality**

| -5 | -4 | -3 | -2 | -1 | 0 | 1 | 2 | 3 | 4 | 5 |

Where are you now?

_____

Where would you like to be?

_____

What are some things you could do right now to help you get where you would like to be?

_____

_____

_____

_____

_____

_____

_____

_____

_____

_____

In what ways are you already working on your connection to your higher self? Complete the sentence, "I would like to acknowledge myself for...." You may have several sentences of acknowledgment.

_____

_____

_____

_____

_____

_____

_____

_____

_____

_____

_____

What old paradigm of thought would you like to release regarding your ego?

_____

_____

_____

_____

_____

_____

_____

_____

_____

_____

_____

_____

How can the ego help you to manifest your intention?

_____

_____

_____

_____

_____

_____

_____

_____

_____

_____

_____

_____

How can you honor the ego and Spiritual nature of everyone you meet without judgment?

_____

_____

_____

_____

_____

_____

_____

_____

_____

_____

_____

_____

What have you learned about yourself through this process?

_____

_____

_____

_____

_____

_____

_____

_____

_____

_____

_____

_____

How can this awareness of what you have learned improve your connection and communication with others?

_____

_____

_____

_____

_____

_____

_____

_____

_____

_____

_____

_____

_____

CHAPTER SIXTEEN

CONFLICT RESOLUTION

Peace cannot be kept by force. It can only be achieved by understanding.
~ Albert Einstein

Even the best of intentions can cause conflict when you least expect it. How does conflict arise? How can we prevent it? We will explore conflict from a humanistic viewpoint based on spirituality and the value each individual brings to the world. To understand how to overcome and prevent conflict is an essential element in the acceptance of your brilliance.

OPTICAL ILLUSIONS

Have you ever seen paintings, drawings, or pictures that appeared to be one image, but when you looked at them differently, you saw a different image? One of the more popular ones depicts what appears to be a young woman but also an old woman. If you don't know at the start that you are looking at a double image, your understanding of that image will depend on what you first see and you probably won't think to look further beyond what you think you see. While you would be correct in your assumption of what you saw, if someone else looked at the same image and saw something else, that person's perspective would be what he or she saw, and both of you would be correct. If asked what the picture was about, you both would state your truths and defend your individual viewpoints based on your individual experiences; thus enters the beginnings of conflict.

KALEIDOSCOPE

Do you remember the colorful wheels you looked at through the viewing tube of a kaleidoscope? As you turned the kaleidoscope, the colors changed.

As adults, we still look through a similar type of instrument, only we now look through our Brilliance Through Balance Wheel, and when we look, we bring with us all our knowledge, experience, success, failure, fear, inspiration, doubt, and memories that have shaped who we are today.

Our life as we know it is viewed through the lens of our Brilliance Through Balance Wheel. As in the optical illusion example above, what you see is your reality. Others view their world through their own Brilliance Through Balance Wheels and that is their reality.

THE INTERSECTION

In traffic, an intersection is where an accident is most likely to occur. Intersections without traffic signals create more challenges because the driver needs to use much more judgment to navigate successfully the intersection. Both instances involve multiple drivers making multiple decisions simultaneously. Although having a license allows us to drive legally, our skill level varies with education and practice.

Whenever people get together, it is similar to traffic at an intersection; when people meet the possibility of an accident, conflict can occur. Each person brings his or her own life experiences to the discussion, and those experiences become the basis for their interpretation of the discussion. Imagine a meeting at work, a discussion with your significant other or children, or talking to someone about politics, religion, or war. Think how easily conflict can occur in these situations without really trying to spark it.

What situations have you encountered where a discussion became a conflict?

_____

_____

_____

_____

_____

_____

_____

_____

THE CRASH = CONFLICT

A crash occurs when one party refuses to accept another's point of view and tries to impose its own view on others. Yes, it's that simple. Sometimes those who are very passionate about an issue get carried away and create the very thing they are fighting against. Think about war protesters who use violence or aggressiveness as a means to get their points across.

The same goes for any discussion you may have where you are passionate about something. It may be with a significant other, a loved one, or in a discussion at work. You can be so passionate that the objectivity becomes lost, and what started out as good intent turns into disagreement, then conflict.

RESOLVING THE CONFLICT

Resolving conflict starts with you rising above the situation and taking the higher road. In resolving conflict, someone has to provide the leadership to move beyond the chaos and into productivity. That person can be you. Here are steps to follow to resolve conflict when it arises.

1. Start by moving from being subjective to objective

Determine what you and the people involved are really trying to accomplish. Leave out words such as like, feel, and believe that have attachment. This step is especially important when emotions run high and passion overrules sensibility.

Moving from subjectivity to objectivity creates a neutral ground conducive to open discussion based on a common goal.

2. Focus on solutions

The tendency may be to go backwards and rehash what happened, who said what, how it was said, and when and why it was said. Instead, focus attention on solving the problem. Focus on the objective determined in Step 1.

If possible, a skilled mediator or facilitator can be an impartial party who can help to keep everyone on track.

Focusing on solutions for couples who are having disagreements can be one of the most effective ways of resolving conflict.

3. Acceptance

Trying to change another person doesn't work. I am not referring to someone who has drug dependency issues, alcohol issues, or other self-destructive behaviors. In these cases, professional help and advice is needed.

Accept individuals for who they are with their unique views, expressions, and what they bring to the world. You do not have to agree with someone else's viewpoint, but you can honor who the person is as an individual and as a Spiritual Being.

4. Release control

Releasing the need to have the world fit into our Brilliance Through Balance Wheel allows us the opportunity to recognize that better ways may exist of doing things, that another person's perspective may shed light, and greater opportunities may unfold as a result of letting go. Release the need to give advice or criticize even under the pretense of "being helpful." Instead, listen to what other people have to say.

5. Let the other party be heard completely

Most conflicts occur when someone feels he or she is not being heard. Release the urge to formulate your response when someone is talking. Instead, listen carefully so you understand and grasp the essence of what is being said. **Find out what is really important to the person speaking.** After the person finishes what he or she has to say, repeat back to the person what you heard to make sure everyone is clear and understands. Start with, "What I heard you say was….Is that correct?"

Repeating what was said anchors that you heard clearly what the other person said and that person will recognize and confirm it, even if the person would prefer to stay antagonistic by feeling no one is listening.

6. Speak from your point of view

When it's your turn to speak, speak from your point of view. Resist the temptation to speak for a group or others. Share your experience while releasing the need to blame, criticize, or give advice. Make it clear you are expressing your own viewpoint. You can say things like, "In my opinion" or "I can't speak for everyone, but here is what would work from my perspective…."

7. Revisit steps 1 and 2

After everyone has had a chance to talk, bring the conversation back to the objective and recap any solutions that have been suggested or begin a dialogue about what can help to resolve the problem at hand.

PERSPECTIVE

How we perceive an event, conversation, image, person or any other thing that enters our life becomes our reality for the moment.

Back in the early '90s, I traveled to Indonesia. Before the trip, I read about the people, culture, and other visitors' experiences. My mind started to formulate an experience about what to expect before I boarded the plane for the long flight to Papua New Guinea, then to Denpasar, Indonesia, the main city on the island of Bali in Indonesia.

Once I arrived and settled in at my hotel, I headed toward the main tourist area where shops lined the streets. A crowd of youngsters bombarded me, trying to sell me handmade gifts, trinkets, and toys so they could make a little money. A price was never set; everything was negotiated. Since I had learned a little of the Indonesian language before reaching Bali, I had fun bartering.

After perusing the shops, I decided to look for where massages were being given on the beach since I had read about them. At that time, it cost $2.50 to have a massage on the beach. I had no idea what to expect as far as the massage's quality or length of time. As I wandered down to the beach, I saw several woman massaging tourists who were lying on mats on the beach; the tourists appeared to be enjoying their massages. I also noticed that while they were being massaged, vendors strolled down the beach selling their wares and stopping by the people being massaged. After being inundated with people trying to sell me things in town, I decided that I wanted a quiet and uninterrupted massage. After a brief negotiation with a masseuse, I asked her to please tell the vendors I was not interested in buying anything. She agreed.

The massage was going well until I was approached by a vendor to buy something. I politely declined and thought I'd just let that one slide as I glanced at the masseuse. I gave her a slightly confused look like, "What's with that? I thought we agreed." Then, wouldn't you know it, another person stopped by to sell me something. Again, I declined, but this time I was irritated. I looked at the woman massaging me and said, "I thought you were going to tell them not to bother me?" In a gentle voice, she said, "They are just trying to sell you something so they can get by."

At that moment, I realized what a selfish tourist I had been. It was all about me and my experience. I had not stopped to think that I had entered a Third World country where the daily minimum wage was $1.07. The people who were lucky enough to have jobs had wages ranging from $29-$234 U.S.D. per month. Yes, per month. Once I understood this fact, I no longer felt irritation toward the vendors, but instead, I understood where they were coming from; their intention was not to annoy me but simply to feed themselves and their families.

Understanding another person's point of view is essential in resolving conflict. Not only does it help to resolve issues, but it validates that person's importance as a fellow Spiritual Being who is on his or her own journey.

PREVENTION IS THE BEST CURE

Why have a head on collision if you can avoid it? Have you ever avoided a collision on the road? You probably were aware of the actions of the other car or had to make a split-second decision and react to the other driver's actions to avoid the accident. Your knowledge, previous experiences, and practice supported you in making the right decisions on the spot.

Following are five ways to help you prevent conflicts:

1. **Balance.** Balance helps to reduce stress and anxiety and allows you to be better prepared and "level-headed" when working or communicating with others. For example, if you have been having arguments with your significant other and have not had much sleep, how would your state of mind and emotions be when working on issues at work, trying to be patient with your kids, or even listening to someone else talk about his problems? Probably not very good. Review your life balance in Chapter 8: Brilliance Through Balance.

2. **Use the Seven Steps to Resolve Conflict.** The seven steps discussed above to resolve conflict can also be used to prevent conflict. If you use them in your daily communications, you will notice a considerable reduction in the number of incidents that might be viewed as unfavorable.

3. **Everyone Has a Story—Respect It!** You never know what a person's life story may be, where he or she has been, was raised, or what had happened to him or her in the

moment before your encounter. Do not accept the surface self the person presents to you; know that everyone
has a deeper, more meaningful connection with his or
her Source of Divine Presence.

4. **Opportunity.** Every encounter you experience is part of
your journey. You have the opportunity to decide whether to follow your heart before you embark on moving
forward. At that decision point, you can prevent conflict
by deciding to look at the situation as a learning experience. Deciding ahead of time that something in that
situation is a learning opportunity positions you to be
open to exploring infinite possibilities rather than closing
down to please the ego self.

5. **Forgiveness.** Let go of past conflicts, disagreements,
hurts, or any other negative feelings that keep you dwelling on how you wish things had been different in the
past. Holding onto those emotions in the present drags
you backwards and prevents you from moving forward
and experiencing the freedom you deserve. Sometimes,
you may need to forgive yourself.

After reading the five steps above, what would you like to
commit to in respect to preventing conflict? Write down your
commitment below. By writing it down, you will make it clear
and your mind will seek to take the commitment and fulfill it.

I, _____, *would like to commit to*

_____

_____

_____

_____

_____

_____

_____

_____

_____

_____

_____

_____

_____   _____

Signature   *Date*

DO NOT CALL LIST

Do you have Caller I.D.? Do you have Caller I.D. to avoid answering calls from solicitors who inundate you with robot-generated messages, or solicitors who will not take "No" for an answer? If by chance a call gets past your screening because you think it may be an important call from someone you know, but it turns out to be a solicitor, how do you feel at that moment? Angry, upset, or @#!!#%*$$!!! mad!

Ask Permission. In this world of instant gratification and in-formation overload, the art of asking permission has gotten lost in the mix. The term "Spam" is no longer used only to mean a meat product, but as a method of sending information to you without permission. Programs are created just to filter out "spam" in the computer world, but somehow, newer and more clever ways are continually created to circumvent the system.

In your daily life, how often do you ask for permission? Asking permission can immediately change the dynamics of a situation and reduce the perception that you are forcing yourself, your ideas, or your ways on someone else. It creates an invitation to be open to what comes next.

SUMMARY: TURNING LEMONS INTO LEMONADE

One time, after I was hired as a sales and marketing manager, I later learned that some of the salespeople already working for the company had hoped to be promoted to the position. The natural progression in most companies is to hire from within, but the president of this company was a very sharp man who thought differently. Although it may have been politically correct to hire from within, he knew that in order to continue his vision, at that time, it was best to find someone from the outside.

After it was officially announced that I was the new sales and marketing manager, I faced many very unhappy people. I received very little support from the sales team, and I knew I had a long road ahead of me. As the economy began its downward cycle, time was not on our side. I had to unify the team quickly to address real business issues.

Among the people upset with my receiving the job was one person in particular, the one who had the most potential to be in the position I had obtained. He let me know loud and clear he was not happy with the turn of events. In fact, he came up to me after the announcement and declared to my face, "Your getting this job over me is not fair to my family." I was shocked! It was as if I had personally done something to destroy his well-being and future.

The very next day, I was equally surprised when he asked to meet with me. When I asked, "Why?" he said he wanted to know my intentions and how he would fit into the picture of what I had in mind. Once we met, I explained to him why I thought he didn't get the job and we had an honest conversation about it. Based on what little I knew about him, I shared with him the value I thought he had to offer to the company at the moment, and then, I offered to help him eventually to get my job.

I ultimately created a position for him that used his strengths and increased his value to the company. Over time, his role also brought notoriety to him as an instrumental person in our business. Years later, as we sat alone, he looked over to me and said, "I thought I wanted your position, but when I see what you have to go through, I realize that what you have me doing is what I love." Working through conflict allowed him to realize what he really loved doing, and it moved him from living in ego to honoring the Spirit within him. It also helped us to communicate and understand one another, and as the years went by, we became good friends.

Conflict can always be resolved as long as you create an environment that is conducive to resolution and prevention. Each resolution brings growth and learning. Each situation provides an opportunity to create deeper meaning, develop closer relationships, and to learn a little more about yourself.

SECTION FIVE

★

ACKNOWLEDGMENT

★

The best and safest thing is to keep a balance in your life, acknowledge the great powers around us and in us. If you can do that, and live that way, you are really a wise man.
~ Euripides

CHAPTER SEVENTEEN

ACKNOWLEDGMENT

Acknowledgment is the gift of recognition.
~ Jeff Bow

Have you ever just wanted to know that you were heard? To know that someone actually was listening to you, valued your opinion, and for a moment, was able to stand in your shoes and see what you were going through? You are not alone.

In the workplace, employees want to know they are valued. Regardless of position, they want to know that they are contributors to the overall success of the company. It's really no different at home. According to Dr. Gabriel Cousins, women want to know they are loved and men want to know they are needed and appreciated. What I learned from Dr. Cousin's Sacred Relationship Class confirmed what I already knew from a business perspective. One of the main reasons why people leave their jobs is from feeling a lack of acknowledgment, an absence of recognition that goes beyond just saying, "Good job."

WHAT IS ACKNOWLEDGMENT?

Acknowledgment is a form of recognition and connection. When done properly, acknowledgment sends a clear message to the recipient that he or she is being heard and is valued. With each acknowledgment comes a better understanding that the acknowledger and the one being acknowledged are creating a space to be better connected.

There are different types of acknowledgments such as the quick, "Yes," "Good Job," "Uh-Huh" or the non-verbal nod, wave, a greeting or even a smile. However, the type of acknowledgment that is being referred to here is specific recognition for the accomplishments achieved, focusing on what is working rather than what is not.

In the sections below, we will look at three forms of acknowledgement:

1. Self-Acknowledgment

2. Acknowledgment by Others

3. Acknowledgment of Others

SELF-ACKNOWLEDGMENT

As a child, I was brought up not to talk about myself. My siblings and I were taught to be humble, to stay in the background, and not to make too much noise. That philosophy stuck with me through the years until I was introduced to a new concept by Peter J. Reding and Marcia Collins of Coach for Life. They introduced a concept of acknowledgment that really helped me to change the way I interpreted, gave, and received compliments. I now view this process of acknowledgment as gift giving and receiving. One of the greatest gifts you can give and receive is self-acknowledgment.

Self-Acknowledgment vs. Bragging. A world of difference exists between bragging and acknowledging. Self-acknowledgment is not about bragging. Bragging is boasting about yourself in a way that serves your ego. Self-acknowledgment is about recognizing areas in your life where you have expressed your innate brilliance through the sharing of your gifts and talents.

Self-acknowledgment helps to build confidence, which in turn helps to break through any fears that creep up as you move forward in your life or business. Acknowledging your successes along the way supports your claim to magnificence at each milestone. Each point of recognition provides an opportunity to mark that point to keep you moving forward in your journey.

Get started. Start to acknowledge yourself by using the words, "I would like to acknowledge myself for...." Following is a scenario you can use as an example. Five times a week, I post information on my Facebook fan page, **www.facebook.com/jeffbowcoaching**, knowing that what I am sharing may or may not resonate with others. Sometimes people make a comment, sometimes they click "Like" if the article resonates with them and they like it, but at other times, I may get no response at all.

Here is an example of a self-acknowledgment: "I would like to acknowledge myself for having the persistence to post continually inspirational messages, quotes, or sayings with the knowing that I am helping to make a positive difference in this world to those who follow, whether or not they comment, "Like," or respond."

You can acknowledge yourself in any part of your life such as in your work, as a parent, spouse, or partner, for how you handle finances, as a homemaker, etc.

Start with two acknowledgments that immediately come to mind.

1. I would like to acknowledge myself for

_____

_____

_____

_____

_____

_____

_____

2. I would like to acknowledge myself for

_____

_____

_____

_____

_____

_____

_____

Add a third acknowledgment. Acknowledge yourself in an area that you are trying to change.

For example: You are having financial difficulties at this time in your life. Acknowledge yourself for what you are already doing to make it better. "I would like to acknowledge myself for taking the first step and reviewing areas where I can improve my finances and possibly save money."

1. I would like to acknowledge myself for

_____

_____

_____

_____

_____

_____

_____

_____

The more you practice self-acknowledgment, the more you will be amazed by the power that unfolds within you. As we discussed in a previous chapter, what we focus on expands. Through acknowledgment of what you are doing right, you will begin to see more opportunities, possibilities, and hope for your success. Self-acknowledgment helps to solidify what you have always known to be true and continues to support you in breaking through fears as they arise.

ACKNOWLEDGMENT BY OTHERS

Growing up in Hawaii was fun. I feel blessed by how Hawaii's diverse mix of cultures allowed me to have multicultural experiences. As an Asian, I had humility instilled in me as a desirable trait. The other cultures in Hawaii also valued this trait so it created a sort of ohana (family) atmosphere and led people not to focus on themselves but to help others without being asked.

Acknowledgments given to us by others were downplayed, and often when a person received acknowledgment, it was pretty common to deny the compliments as being true. It is also very common in Hawaii for gifts, such as food, to be given to thank someone for helping. After the receiver says many, "You shouldn't have's," the gift is finally accepted. Commonly, barbecues or cookouts took place after an event as a mass "Thank you" to everyone who helped out, and as an excuse to party.

Receiving. For many of us, it is easier to accept a thank you gift than it is to accept a compliment. However, I've come to realize that when I receive an acknowledgment or compliment, I am allowing the other person to give. When we deny recognition offered to us by saying anything other than "Thank you," it's as if we are taking a gift handed to us and dropping it at the other person's feet. Receiving the gift for what it is allows the person giving it to be heard and acknowledged so he or she can feel complete.

Receiving allows us to be a better giver. It allows the circulation of energy inside us that helps to reenergize our Spirit and to continue sharing our gifts and talents with the world. Without receiving, we may eventually burn out, be unhappy, and at some point, embody a negative attitude without even knowing it. We may still put on a smiling face, but inside, we may slowly be yearning for appreciation and validation.

Practice. When someone pays you a compliment or acknowledges you, respond with a simple "Thank you." Take a moment to accept and appreciate the gift that is being given; enjoy being in that moment.

ACKNOWLEDGMENT OF OTHERS

Wouldn't it be nice if you were acknowledged for your contributions at work or home? As you begin to acknowledge others, you will be amazed by how it shifts and changes your energy. Furthermore, what we recognize in others reflects the traits we have ourselves. As I said earlier, "If you spot it, you've got it."

By acknowledging others, you will recognize the things you have done and accomplished. You will be able to look back and be proud of how far you have come. With this energy, you will continually close the gap for fear to sneak in.

Acknowledgment of others is when you recognize their talents and gifts and share that observation with them. It is always best to acknowledge someone close to the time when you witness the person's magnificence in action. This timing will lead to the recipient having a greater connection linking your acknowledgment to his or her actions. The closer the time of your acknowledgment to the person's actions, the higher the impact.

Acknowledgment goes far beyond the conciliatory, "Good job," "Nice," or "Well done." Impactful acknowledgment contains these characteristics:

1. It comes from your perspective of what you witnessed as the person's brilliance.

2. It is specific in nature, timely, and genuine.

3. It connects the person, his or her action, and the result.

Example Scenario: You just noticed that John did an amazing job completing a project with Jill, a very difficult client who was thinking about switching companies. John's actions turned the relationship around, and not only did he retain the client, but now Jill is referring other potential clients to John's company.

Example Acknowledgment: "John, I really would like to acknowledge you for the way you handled the project with Jill. I was impressed by how you took a difficult situation and skillfully worked with her to turn it around. Your patience was amazing. You took the time to let her settle down when she was upset, and you worked with her to find out what was important to her that the rest of us were missing. As a result, not only did you save Jill as a client, but now she is referring a lot of potential clients to us. Brilliant!"

In the example above, look at the specific words used, and write out what words correspond to the different elements of acknowledging someone. By writing out the words chosen, it will help to solidify what you are learning about acknowledgment.

What words convey that the acknowledgment comes from your perspective of what you witnessed in the person's brilliance?

_____

_____

_____

_____

_____

_____

_____

_____

What words convey that the acknowledgment is specific in nature, timely, and genuine?

_____

_____

_____

_____

_____

_____

_____

_____

_____

_____

What words are used to connect John to his action and the results?

_____

_____

_____

_____

_____

_____

_____

_____

_____

_____

Now think about other times when you have witnessed someone do something extraordinary and brilliant. You may or may not have acknowledged that person at the time, but using the questions above, think about what words you used or could have used to acknowledge them.

THE POWER OF ACKNOWLEDGMENT

Imagine the results from using acknowledgment with coworkers, people you lead, your bosses, your children, your family, the server at a restaurant, or the clerk helping you at a store. You can make someone's day every day by acknowledging him or her.

As discussed in Chapter 10: The Circle Theory, the compounding effects that can ripple out are phenomenal. If you influence someone's life positively, that person is likely in turn to influence someone else, and the positive ripple effect may reach five to seven people. The more someone is exposed to the concept of receiving acknowledgment, the sooner it will become a consistent part of his or her life.

The power of acknowledgment can intentionally be used when developing a culture/brand for a business, teamwork, teaching, or creative development. The possibilities are endless.

WHAT IF A RECEIVER OF ACKNOWLEDGMENT DOESN'T GET IT?

It is very possible that the receiver might not get your acknowledgment for several reasons. He might not understand due to cultural differences or because it is a new concept to him, or he may have seen poor recognition attempts before that didn't last.

I have experienced this situation firsthand with my mother. She is a first generation Chinese immigrant who loves her children and would do anything within her means to help them before she did anything for herself. Our family is not a touchy, feely one that shares its emotions, but we feel one another's unconditional love through our interactions.

One time, after having been away for a long time traveling, I visited my mom to see how she was doing. She cooked a delicious meal for me, so after the meal, I thought I would acknowledge her. After I thanked her for taking the time to cook one of my favorite meals, she said, "What's wrong with you? I'm your mother. Why are you thanking me?"

One has to keep being who he or she is, so it may be hard for a person to accept acknowledgment at first, but if you keep acknowledging the person, eventually acknowledgment will not be a new concept to the person; he or she will get used to it so it will become a new part of who that person is; the person will also feel appreciated and express appreciation more often to others, I still thank my mom regularly, and she has come to accept the gift of receiving. I guess it just rubs off after a while.

SUMMARY

Continuing to acknowledge your successes along the way will bring you more success in the future. Acknowledging your brilliance builds confidence, minimizes fear, and eventually, supports you to break through it.

You will be amazed by what you will discover when you look for things to acknowledge about yourself and others. Your focus will be geared toward what is working, positive, and motivating. You are the creator of your own destiny. You are brilliant. You are loved.

★ CHAPTER EIGHTEEN ★

GRATITUDE

Gratitude makes sense of our past, brings peace for today,
and creates a vision for tomorrow.
~ Anonymous

We have much to be thankful for in this lifetime. Gratitude is the recognition of the grace of God (or your Source of Divine Presence).

Is it possible to focus on what is working in your life every day?

One of the great gifts we have right now that does not cost anything is the ability to choose. We can choose which clothes to wear today, what to eat for breakfast, lunch, or dinner, and we can choose happiness. We make hundreds of more choices every day without thinking about them, even choices we may later blame on others, such as the choice to be miserable, grumpy, or mean.

Perhaps the most important choice we can make is to look for things in our lives that are working and to be grateful for them. We can acknowledge and appreciate everything good that comes to us by expressing our gratitude for it. When we recognize what is working in our lives, we allow spirit to work through us rather than letting our ego deceive us about our true nature.

Primarily celebrated in the U.S. and Canada, Thanksgiving is a day set aside to give thanks to God. Initially, the holiday began in 1621 when the Wampanoag Indians and the English colonists at Plymouth, Massachusetts came together to share their harvest in the form of a feast. In 1863, Thanksgiving became a national holiday in the United States. The holiday has come down to us as a symbol of cooperation among people and a time to be grateful for all the blessings in our lives.

ONCE IS NOT ENOUGH

Holidays bring awareness to a special time or event. My experience has been that after a holiday celebration, most people go back to their normal lives, and a week later, the only thing they remember is how much they ate, how much they drank, and how they partied. Over time, the real meaning of such events becomes diluted and commercialized by the mainstream. At the same time, others, in their grass roots efforts, attempt to perpetuate the true meaning and value of what was originally created.

I remember watching an episode of *The Oprah Winfrey Show*, where Oprah talked about keeping a gratitude journal. A gratitude journal is reserved specifically for writing down three things we are grateful for every day before we go to bed. As I watched Oprah talk about a gratitude journal, I thought it was a great way to exercise the ability to focus on what is working in our lives and to be thankful for it every day. By keeping a gratitude journal, we consciously acknowledge the abundance in our lives and it helps to commit the many reasons we have to feel gratitude to memory.

COMMIT TO FINDING SPIRIT IN EVERY SITUATION, EVERYDAY!

Every day we can commit to keeping our own gratitude journals. It only takes a minute or two to review the day and think about the good things that happened for which we are grateful. As an example, here's a great quote by celebrity Michael J. Fox about what gives him reason to be grateful. Fox has lived with Parkinson's disease, for many years, but rather than focus on what is wrong in his life, he focuses on what is right—what makes him grateful:

I wake up curious every day and every day I'm surprised by something. And if I can just recognize that surprise every day and say, "Oh, that's a new thing, that's a new gift that I got today that I didn't even know about yesterday," it keeps me going. It keeps me more than going. It keeps me enthusiastic and grateful.
~ Michael J. Fox

Now it's your turn to commit daily to a gratitude journal:

I, _____, commit myself to start looking for things to be grateful for every day. Every day I will find three or more things, people, or events that I am thankful for in my life. I know that everything is perfect and my life is evolving as it should. When I am grateful, I am connected to my Source of Divine Presence.

I will write down my thoughts of thankfulness and keep them for the times when I get off track and have a hard day, a bumpy road, or a perceived setback. My gratitude journal will remind me what wisdom and freedom exist when I am connected to my Source of Divine Presence. In this state of gratitude, I am at my most powerful, and I can acknowledge my brilliance as I let Spirit shine through me.

I am grateful!

_____   _____

Signature   *Date*

If you do not already have a journal you can use, begin by writing down the things for which you are grateful now and you can transfer them to your gratitude journal later.

Today, _____ (Date), I am grateful for:

1. _____
2. _____
3. _____

POWER THROUGH THE POTHOLES

It's easy to be grateful when everything is going well, we have our health, friends, and family around us, and a job. But what about those times when we are struggling, out of work, or have encountered a tragic event?

It's okay to let ourselves just "be" at times. At other times, it's even okay to give ourselves permission to waddle in our misery, to grieve, be frustrated, or vent to get it out of our system. In some situations, we may be able to move forward immediately just as we would keep driving if we ran over a pothole. And if we have a flat tire, we fix it, and move on.

Unforeseen circumstances will always occur in our lives just as sure as the sun rises and sets. The unexpected is a part of life on earth, and we are woven into a fabric of oneness in love, consciousness, and caring whether we realize it or not at the time. We see examples of this closeness in times of tragedy, such as the attack on the World Trade Center, Hurricane Katrina, or the tidal wave in Thailand. People are brought together through common causes, and an outpouring of empathy and love arises.

Mexico has thousands of potholes. If you tell the locals there that you ran over a pothole, they will reply, "Why did you run over the pothole?" To them, it's not only funny, but it is only common sense that if you can see the pothole, you can avoid it. If you cannot avoid it, you are driving too fast or too close to the car in front of you.

We are emotional beings with five, and some say six, senses that allow us to live vibrant lives. When change occurs in a form other than what we expect, it disrupts our lives on an emotional level. At some point, we have to accept it, whether we agree with it or not, and move on. Finding value, a lesson, or the gift in the experience, and knowing that everything happens as it should will help you to move forward in challenging times.

Who are you grateful for at this moment in your life?

1. _____   2. _____

3. _____   4. _____

5. _____   6. _____

7. _____   8. _____

9. _____   10. _____

NO BETTER TIME THAN NOW

Gratitude supports you to be in the present by recognizing those things that are working. Even when things are emotionally taxing, gratitude can bring peace and love forward to help you through those times. There is never a better time than the present to express your gratitude.

Let the ten people listed above know how grateful you are by calling them, meeting them in person, emailing them, or by sending them a handwritten card to express your gratitude for their being in your life. There is no better time than now to express your gratitude.

THANK YOU

I would like to express my gratitude to you the reader. I appreciate your investing your time and money to buy this book, but more importantly, to invest in yourself. I am grateful that you have made it this far through the book, and that you have not given up on reading it or on improving your life. You are breaking through your fears and igniting your brilliance.

CHAPTER NINETEEN

INSPIRATION

Anyone can give up; it's the easiest thing in the world to do.
But to hold it together when everyone else would understand if
you fell apart, that's true strength.
~ Author Unknown

Do you believe there is a Higher Power or Source greater than yourself? Whatever your answer is to this question, you are correct. Your answer is a reflection of your thoughts and feelings. That Higher Power or greater Source is the ultimate source of inspiration; it reflects our faith in something greater than ourselves that guides us, and our faith in something that allows us to become greater and to do extraordinary things.

While motivation comes from an external source that influences you in some way, inspiration births from within and triggers a shift, an action, or a power to move the intellect or emotions. The roots of the word stem from a meaning to do something "in Spirit" or "under the influence of the Spirit." In other words, inspiration and inspired actions come from our connection to our Source of Divine Presence.

YOU INSPIRE ME…REALLY?

As with happiness, many people believe that inspiration comes from a place other than within themselves. However, when we feel motivated to do something, it is usually someone or something else that convinces us that to take action would be a good idea. Motivational speakers are great and serve an amazing purpose in this world. It would be interesting, however, to find statistics upon how many people, after hearing a motivational speaker, watching a motivational movie, or reading a motivational book, truly take action based on that motivation. Wouldn't it be great if motivation, being an outside source, were equivalent to getting your oil changed in your car? Everyone who goes to the garage and pays for an oil changes leaves with the oil changed in the car—a 100 percent success rate. Unfortunately, motivation isn't that effective. We can have a motivational speaker give us all the tools to succeed, but a shift has to occur within us to make us agree to make the changes necessary or to take the actions required for that dream to become reality. Inspiration is that connection with Source that encourages us to take action. Something external may motivate us, but all the motivation in the world will be of no use if we don't feel inspired to act.

IT'S ALL ABOUT YOU

The connection that determines and drives inspiration is a subjective one. It is determined by your likes, dislikes, opinions, beliefs, experiences, situations, and a combination of all of these. A wealthy person who attends a financial seminar titled, "How I Made My Millions" may not find it as motivating as someone who is looking for financial freedom. Therefore, the wealthy person may not be as inspired to take action as someone wanting financial freedom.

Inspiration is like a burst of caffeine, an adrenaline rush, or an endorphin high. Its effects may have a short or long duration, depending on the quality of the connection and the follow up to the inspiration, as we discussed in Section 3: Action.

OUTER INFLUENCES THAT TRIGGER INTERNAL REACTIONS

At certain times in life, you may come across something, someone, or a situation that just clicks. It sets off a response that moves you. You may have encountered a painting, a poem, trees, Nature, a documentary, music, or people who may have moved and inspired you on the spot. You make a connection with the object of your inspiration that allows you to see infinite possibilities, and that connection causes you to change your thinking or your emotions. When you put yourself in situations that resonate with who you are, you create an atmosphere that is motivating and conducive to connecting to your Source of Divine Presence. Connecting to this Source lends itself to inspiration.

What are some of the things that have inspired you in the past?

_____

_____

_____

_____

_____

_____

_____

Here is a list of people who have inspired me:

1. The 14th Dalai Lama

The Dalai Lama's book *The Art of Happiness: A Handbook for Living* presents a message that resonated with me because it is simple and to the point: we are all, ultimately, striving for happiness.

2. Bob Hope and Dolores Reade

Bob Hope and Dolores Reade had a sixty-nine year marriage. During their lifetimes, more than half of all marriages ended in divorce, and the entertainment industry's marriage success rate varied as much as the weather, yet Bob and Dolores managed to find a way to make it work.

3. Joel Osteen

Joel is a pastor at Lakewood Church. He took over the ministry after his father fell ill. Joel first caught my attention when I was channel surfing and stopped to hear him talk on his television show. I was impressed by his positive message and his openness to all people. He was funny and entertaining, and he provided real life stories I could relate to my own life.

Although I am not of any particular religious affiliation and embrace all people and faiths that do not harm others, Osteen's style of delivery and what he stands for inspired me. He has had his share of criticism, but he still maintains his path of what he believes to be true and how he communicates that to make a positive difference in people's lives.

4. Shirley Anderson

Shirley Anderson is a Master Certified Coach. Early in my own career as a coach, I attended an International Coaching Conference where she offered a breakout session. One thing she said in her workshop that has always stayed with me was, "We lose too many good coaches who are trying to make it in this business. Do not give up. If you have to get a job to pay the bills while you build your practice, get a job. But never stop calling yourself a coach."

5. All people who are passionate and living their dreams

I love it when I hear someone say, "It doesn't feel like work because it is so much fun" or "I wouldn't want to be doing anything else." Those words draw me in and make me want to learn more about the person, his or her business, and how he or she got started. Many successful people had very humble beginnings and started off very small. That they overcome some big obstacles to succeed inspires me.

Who are three people who have inspired you?

1. _____

2. _____

3. _____

KEEPING THE MOMENTUM GOING

Now that we are close to the end of this book, it's important to emphasize that you must keep the momentum going. If you have been doing all the exercises and reflecting on your journey, you may encounter a lull in the process once you finish this book. If you do, here are some ideas that may help:

1. Find a mentor or coach to support you.

2. Research someone you admire, trust, and resonate with who has accomplished what you desire. Extract the things he or she has done that you find may work for you and implement them.

3. Go easy on yourself. Sometimes you can push yourself to a point to achieve a goal, but you end up unhappy in the end. Be kind to yourself and others when a mistake is made. Work toward solutions.

4. Acknowledge your successes along the way.

5. Be persistent.

As the leader in your life and business, your inspiration provides motivation to others. The great energy aura that surrounds an inspired person or business is contagious. It can rapidly transform the dull and mundane into the exhilarating, the lackluster to brilliant, poor performance to superstardom, and from being a follower to being a leader in your industry.

SUMMARY

Inspiration acknowledges passion and purpose and brings it immediately to the forefront of your life. It creates a vehicle to move you forward, and it allows you continually to express your gifts and talents.

Inspiration is the spark that ignites your brilliance and continues to energize you as you pursue your vision and dreams.

Never, ever, give up. Continually remind yourself of the things that inspire you. They may include your vision board, a painting, your gratitude journal, or whatever creates inspiration for you to keep going. Keep focused on where you want to be with the end result in mind.

CHAPTER TWENTY

LOVE

The power of love has no limits or boundaries. All possibilities exist with love because it is infinite.
~ Jeff Bow

This chapter summarizes the true essence of the process this book has taken you through, in one word: Love. Love is the basis of all creation because it brings new life into this world. Not just physical birthing of life but also the unfolding of self as your consciousness changes and you gain greater insight into your spiritual growth.

One of the greatest gifts you can give and receive is the love of self. If you are open to the understanding that you can love yourself beyond judgment, then you can explore the beauty of what love has to offer. In the receiving of love, you can recognize your brilliance and your Source of Divine Presence as you become the conduit to spread love through your gifts and talents.

Acknowledgment of this love anchors your place in the world. As you move to your next vision, juicier dreams and new adventures, it is with confidence and fearlessness—fearlessness in the sense that you know all things work out for the best.

Love is perhaps the only thing in life that is unconditional. The only conditions it has are those we place on it or let others place on it.

THE ART OF BEING HUMAN

After all is said and done, we are human beings. Complete with feelings, emotions, and an ego. The most difficult part of love happens when we become attached to love and selfishly want to keep what we associate with it forever. It's natural to feel these emotions and attachments. It often happens when a person or pet passes away, a break up occurs, or through the loss of a job. These emotions also appear at times when we feel we are being tested to see whether what we are offering is true love.

I have found the paradox, that if you love until it hurts, there can be no more hurt, only more love.
~ Mother Teresa

If we truly believe love never dies, then is it the tangible evidence in a physical form to which we are attached? Is it our perception of a redefined relationship that masks itself as a new interpretation of love? Whatever the case may be, experiencing emotion is necessary to experiencing love. If we love completely and unselfishly, we will experience love in its greatest form, regardless of whatever earthly conditions are placed upon it.

The art of being human balances the body, mind, and spirit. It unites these dynamics into a comprehensive Oneness that allows the experience of life to unfold as it should through love. Love's power is then undeniable; its gifts incredible; its reach infinite.

Through the mist of curiosity is a reflection of light that is the true expression of Oneness.
~ Jeff Bow

YOU ARE THE DIFFERENCE

We need have no doubt that the world will unfold as it should. The complex mix of brilliance that shines on earth is the result of increased collective consciousness that moves this world. Each individual has an opportunity to reach his or her highest potential of happiness, fulfillment, and joy. In doing so, a person increases the lumen count and allows others to do the same.

Sometimes giving yourself and others the space to be who they are and to live their dreams is not easy. In fact, it can be uncomfortable, scary, and even hurt at times. Instead, when you embrace the unknown and have faith that all things happen for the best, you create for yourself a security blanket that increases your connection to Source.

Your need to be right is a direct reflection of your need to be loved.
~ Jeff Bow

Your life should not be static. That's why it's called living. If you are not living, you are just existing. If you just exist in this world, you are letting others define your quality of happiness.

You have within you, right now, everything you need to take charge of your own happiness and not let fear get in the way. Stop thinking, and start believing. Break through fear and ignite your brilliance. Be true to yourself, to the brilliance within you. When you are true to yourself, you are respecting yourself, and you are respecting others by trusting them with seeing the real you. When you embody the values that make you who you are and you represent what you stand for, you stand in your truth; you have integrity. At that moment, you present to the world the greatest gift you can ever possibly give.

THE POWER OF LOVE

One of the most powerful stories I have ever heard was on MSN[1] titled, "Mom's hug revives baby after being pronounced dead." Kate and David Ogg were told that one of their twins, Jamie, died shortly after birth. Jamie was placed on Kate's chest so she could say her last goodbyes. As she gently stroked and talked to Jamie for two hours, he began to gasp for air. As this continued, the doctors told the parents not to get their hopes up. Nevertheless, Jamie came back to life. Jamie lived because of the magic of his mother's touch and the power of her love.

REFLECTIONS

Take the time to write down your thoughts, feelings, ideas, or anything that may have come up for you in this chapter. You may wish to reflect on the power of love in your own life and

1 You can watch the interview of this remarkable story at http://today.msnbc. msn.com/id/38988444/ns/today-parenting/

when it has made a difference, or places where you think showing more love might help one of your relationships.

_____

_____

_____

_____

_____

_____

_____

_____

_____

_____

_____

_____

_____

_____

_____

_____

_____

_____

_____

_____

_____

_____

_____

_____

_____

_____

★

A FINAL NOTE

Thank you for taking the time to read this book. It is one of many books and resources that can support you on this wonderful journey we call life. Now that you have finished, ask yourself these questions: "With all the information I have now, what will I do differently tomorrow?" and "Who can help to keep me accountable to myself to live the life I have always dreamed of having?"

You have a choice to carry on with your life as it currently is and to keep your dreams in your back pocket. Or, you can take action and start to live a naturally vibrant life—one filled with joy, happiness, and love.

Our lives are ever changing and evolving. There may be a point in your life that can be considered "life changing," but it is all of your experiences that collectively form the magnificent person you are today.

My wish is that in some way this book has inspired you to take action, not settle for less, and to know you can make a positive difference in your life and this world.

Namaste,

★

ADDITIONAL RESOURCES

BOOKS

Collins, Jim and Jerry Porras. *Built to Last: Successful Habits of Visionary Companies*. New York: HarperCollins, 1994.

Dalai Lama. *The Art of Happiness: A Handbook for Living*. New York: Riverhead Books, 1998.

Fox, Emmett. *Power Through Constructive Thinking*. New York: HarperOne, 1989.

Frankl, Victor. *Man's Search for Meaning*. 1959. Boston: Beacon Press, 2006.

Hay, Louise. *You Can Heal Your Life*. Carlsbad, CA: Hay House, 1999.

Keith, Sam. *One Man's Wilderness: An Alaskan Odyssey*. 1973. Portland, OR: Alaska Northwest Books, 1999.

Langer, Ellen J. *Mindfulness*. n.p.: Perseus Books, 1989.

Nhat Hanh, Thich. *Living Buddha, Living Christ*. New York: Riverhead Books, 1995.

Pausch, Randy. *The Last Lecture*. New York: Hyperion Books, 2008.

Shaiman, Barbara Greenspan. *Live Your Legacy Now*. Bloomington, IN: iUniverse, 2009.

FILMS

Alone in the Wilderness. Dir. Bob Swerer. With Dick Proenneke. 2003.

The Secret. Dir. Drew Heriot et al. With Bob Proctor, Joe Vitale et al. 2006.

What the Bleep Do We Know?!. Dir. William Arntz et al. With Marlee Matlin, Elaine Hendrix, and John Ross Bowie. 2004.

★

ACKNOWLEDGMENTS

WITH LOVE AND GRATITUDE

I would like to acknowledge my family members who have supported me in my life's work.

Nora: For touching my life in more ways than you could have ever imagined. You are a Radiant Star!

Mom, Mike, Gail, and Tara: I could not have asked to be born into a better family.

Dad: May this book connect us through Spirit and make you proud of who I have become and what I stand for in this world.

Tim and Carla: Thank you for giving me the gift of experiencing what it might have been like to have my own children. You are special to me and I am so proud of both of you.

My Clients: I would like to acknowledge and thank my clients for the privilege to support you on your path. May you continue to make a positive difference in this world.

Peter J. Reding and Marcia Collins: I am forever grateful for being led to Coach for Life and for meeting you both. You have made such a positive difference in my life and the lives of so many others in this world. Thank you!!!

Patrick Snow: Thank You! Not only are you a great writing coach but someone I call a friend. Without you, this book never would have been published.

Tyler Tichelaar: Thank you for your outstanding work in making sure that my intended message is conveyed properly in my writing.

Fusion Creative Works: The amazing cover rocks! Thank you.

Jeff Langcaon: Thank you for your outstanding work with the illustrations.

To everyone I have had the pleasure to cross paths with in this lifetime, I thank you. The culmination of those encounters and experiences has helped to shape who I am today.

★

ABOUT THE AUTHOR

JEFF BOW

**Executive and Leadership Coach to Those
Who Seek More Satisfaction and Balance in Their Lives**

BRILLIANCE THROUGH BALANCE™

Executives from Los Angeles, Hawaii, and Shanghai consider their twice monthly private coaching calls with Master Certified Life Coach Jeff Bow to be among the best ongoing investments they make to continue their success and satisfaction in business and life. Jeff's proprietary Brilliance through Balance™ approach is the reason clients say they achieve their goals faster, enjoy life a lot more, and feel more deeply connected to Spirit.

Jeff believes, and **his clients agree**, that the deep sense of purpose that flows from setting priorities in concert with what matters most for each person is the fuel that drives inspired growth in every aspect of our lives. **Spirituality is at the center of this work, as opposed to being just one essential ingredient in the success mix.** Most clients work with Jeff over a year-long period to welcome remarkable results and rewards that are priceless in their lasting value.

THREE DECADES OF IMPACT

Not a stranger to long-term commitments, Jeff worked for three decades as a strategic change agent for organizations ranging from a magazine and book distributor to a construction material manufacturer and supplier before launching his successful private executive coaching practice in 2003. In this role, Jeff's gifts and talents for shaping company cultures to honor mutual respect and the celebration of the Human Spirit were well-honed. He was proud to put to rest antiquated leadership philosophies such as, "Do as I say; not as I do" in order to open up new, collaborative work styles that bring about stunning, revenue-generating results and team satisfaction.

While Jeff has made a lot of hard business decisions, negotiated contracts, and fought for workers' rights to make a lasting difference for leading organizations, one of the hardest personal decisions he ever made was putting Kila, his treasured nine-year old Rottweiler, to sleep. Doing what was best for Kila, after considering what would be Kila's quality of life with bone cancer versus Kila resting peacefully, put into poignant focus for Jeff the importance of remembering Spirit first.

One of Jeff's favorite quotes, which he could apply to that situation, is:

The ultimate measure of a man is not where he stands in moments of comfort and convenience, but where he stands at times of challenge and controversy.
~ Martin Luther King

Today, Jeff connects deeply with high performing executives to guide their most inspired performances and to help them increase their satisfaction in their work and lives. In his non-judgmental, receptive, and nurturing way, Jeff supports and motivates clients to guide their teams to accomplishing more than they ever thought possible, while showing them how to welcome more joy, fulfillment, and positive results into their own lives.

JEFF'S EDUCATION AND CREDENTIALS

Jeff is a Master Certified Life Coach, an inspired learning facilitator, and a graduate of the accredited Coach for Life program. He is an active member of the International Coach Federation, and he earned a certificate from Stanford University Graduate School of Business in its Executive Program for Growing Companies. Jeff also completed coursework in negotiation for the senior executives program via the Inter-University Consortium of Harvard University, Massachusetts Institute of Technology, and Tufts University.

JEFF'S PUBLICATIONS AND MEDIA CONTRIBUTIONS

Jeff has appeared on Joni B. Redick-Yundt's *Million Dollar Attitude* television show on the episode "Guarantee Your Success!" He contributed his expertise to a Harvard Business School research study of the executive coaching profession, the results of which were published as "The Realities of Executive Coaching" in the January 2009 issue of the *Harvard Business Review*.

Jeff welcomes media interviews and speaking invitations from professional groups and associations that seek to benefit from his Brilliance through Balance™ message and overall approach.

To learn more and to engage with Jeff, visit him at:

www.JeffBowCoaching.com

www.ingramcontent.com/pod-product-compliance
Lightning Source LLC
Chambersburg PA
CBHW060258100426
42742CB00011B/1792